Train to Progress

Repeat for Success

An easy to use book of Showjumping exercises to make training sessions creative, beneficial and motivating.

Suitable for both coaches and riders.

Mandy Frost
Showjumping Coach

© Mandy Frost 2020

All rights reserved. No part of this publication may be reproduced or transmitted in any form or by any means, electronic or mechanical, including photocopy, recording or any information storage and retrieval system, without permission in writing from the author.

The right of Mandy Frost to be identified as the author of this work has been asserted by her in accordance with the Copyright, Designs and Patents Act 1988.

The author shall have neither liability nor responsibility to any person or entity with respect to any loss or damage caused, or alleged to be caused, directly or indirectly by the information contained in this book.

First edition published 2020 in English

ISBN 978-1-5272-6502-8

Acknowledgements

I would like to thank Emma Richardson and Nicky Fuller for their constant support and enthusiasm throughout the production of this book. Your help and guidance has been extremely significant in relation to the outcome of this project.

I am also grateful for my family's motivational support and patience while I spent hours transforming my hand-drawn exercises into digital illustrations.

Contents

Introduction……………………………………………………7	Exercise 10 Straightness and square turns…………49
Before You Start………………………………………………9	Exercise 10a Straightness and square turns…………50
Distances Table……………………………………………11	Exercise 11 Straightness and square turns…………51
Tips for Coaches and Riders…………………………13	Exercise 11a Straightness and square turns………52
Keys for Diagrams…………………………………………15	Exercise 12 Accurate circles and suppleness………53
Exercise 1 Straightness………………………………………17	Exercise 12a Accurate circles to poles/jumps……..54
Exercise 1a Straightness……………………………………18	Exercise 12b Accurate circles to poles/jumps……..55
Exercise 1b Straightness……………………………………19	Exercise 12c Castle exercise for suppleness…………56
Exercise 2 Straightness and transitions……………20	Exercise 12d Suppleness and concentration……….57
Exercise 2a Straightness in canter……………………21	Exercise 13 90 degree turns and straightness……58
Exercise 2b Straightness and circles………………22	Exercise 13a 90 degree turns and straightness……59
Exercise 2c Straightness and diagonal lines…………23	Exercise 13b 90 degree turns and straightness……60
Exercise 2d Turning back to straight lines…………24	Exercise14 Riding turn backs and square turns….61
Exercise 3 Riding accurate diagonal lines……………25	Exercise 14a Riding turn backs and square turns….62
Exercise 3a Riding accurate diagonal lines…………26	Exercise 15 Riding angles……………………………………63
Exercise 3b Riding accurate diagonal lines…………27	Exercise 15a Riding angles……………………………………64
Exercise 4 Shortening and lengthening………………28	Exercise 15b Riding angles……………………………………65
Exercise 4a Straightness and circles……………………29	Exercise 16 Riding angles within a course……………66
Exercise 4b Straightness, diagonals/circles…………30	Exercise 17 Planning ahead for multiple angles…..67
Exercise 4c Straightness and accurate turns………31	Exercise 17a Planning ahead for alternate angles…68
Exercise 5 Riding accurate lines…………………………32	Exercise 17b Planning ahead for alternate angles…69
Exercise 5a Riding accurate lines…………………………33	Exercise 18 Alternating turn backs/ transitions….70
Exercise 5b Riding accurate lines…………………………34	Exercise 18a Alternating turn backs……………………71
Exercise 6 Increasing suppleness…………………………35	Exercise 19 Preparing for jump off turns……………72
Exercise 6a Suppleness/variation in canter…………36	Exercise 20 Preparing for jump offs……………………73
Exercise 6b Increasing suppleness and collection..37	Exercise 21 Riding the bending line……………………74
Exercise 6c Increasing suppleness and collection..38	Exercise 21a Riding the bending line……………………75
Exercise 7 Serpentines/figure of 8……………………39	Exercise 21b Riding the bending line……………………76
Exercise 7a Serpentine/figure of 8………………………40	Exercise 22 Turning back to the straight line………77
Exercise 7b Serpentine/figure of 8………………………41	Exercise 22a Turning back to the straight line………78
Exercise 7c Serpentine/figure of 8/circles……………42	Exercise 23 Engaging the canter/accurate lines…79
Exercise 7d Serpentine with bounces……………………43	Exercise 23a Engaging the canter/accurate lines…80
Exercise 8 Riding transitions and diagonals…………44	Exercise 24 Riding with precision………………………81
Exercise 9 Straightness across the diagonal………45	Exercise 25 Riding with precision………………………82
Exercise 9a Straightness on the centre line…………46	Exercise 25a Riding with precision………………………83
Exercise 9b Riding accurate circles………………………47	Exercise 25b Riding with precision………………………84
Exercise 9c Riding accurate circles………………………48	

Introduction

Mandy is a British Showjumping UKCC Level 4 coach, and recently completed a MSc Professional Practice in Sports Coaching. Having previously produced horses from novice to international level she now focuses on coaching both youths and adults, looking to nurture, motivate, challenge and inspire riders to achieve their full potential.

Since starting her coaching career, Mandy has been awarded British Showjumping Coach of the Year, been selected for the Excel Talent Coaching Programme and also for the Youth Coaching Programme.

"Coaching and showjumping are my passion, they make me who I am; motivated, driven and dedicated to empower and improve both horse and rider".

Since the start of my coaching career I have been fascinated with the impact correct training can have on progression and achievement. So, being intent on learning, I would often draw exercises from the day's coaching, making notes on how well they worked, how they might be developed, and how they could be varied in difficulty. Constantly looking back on these drawings made sure my coaching had purpose and meaning, encouraging me to be creative and experiment with new ideas. I often shared these hand-drawn sketches with other coaches, and it was these fellow coaches who motivated me to develop this book.

The content of this book is a mixture of tried and tested exercises, some of which I have created myself and some inspired by other coaches. The goal was to create an easy to use book for coaches and riders, making training sessions beneficial and motivating for both the rider and the horse. Each exercise has step-by-step instructions, making clear the 'aims' of the exercise and includes 'Coach's tips'. You can use different layouts to work on straightness, riding turns, planning ahead, smooth transitions and many other skills to help you progress with your training. All the exercises are suitable for both horses and ponies, and a guide for distances is included to help with setting up the layout.

This book aspires to help you ride with precision, improving the horse's way of going using the following scales of training:

- Rhythm
- Suppleness
- Impulsion
- Straightness
- Collection
- Communication

So before you start

Here are some **training tips** and **skills** to learn that are essential to the success of your sessions:

1. **Loosening up**
   Your horse must always be given the chance to stretch and warm up the muscles before asking him to work in an outline. If your horse is too fresh or not loosened up enough your training session will be less productive.

2. **Leg- yielding**
   When leg-yielding you move the horse forward diagonally with horse flexed away from the direction of movement.

   Aids for leg-yielding
   The aids for the leg yield require communication between the inside aids and the outside aids. The inside leg asks the horse to yield to the side while the outside leg asks the horse to continue forward, maintaining straightness. The inside rein asks for slight flexion in the opposite direction of travel while the outside rein helps maintain straightness and tempo. The rider's position should be balanced slightly over the inside hip with the shoulders square with the horse's shoulders. The inside leg remains at the girth with the outside leg slightly behind the girth, to prevent the haunches from swinging too far to the side.

3. **Half-halt**
   The goal of the half-halt is to re-balance the horse and prepare him for the next movement, whether it is change of direction, transition to a different gait, increasing collection, or even halting completely.

   Aids for half-halt
   Sit tall, with your neck, shoulders and arms relaxed and tighten your core muscles. Close your legs to support the horse and press the horse forward into your hands, remembering to keep the horse's energy active. Restrict the forward motion by closing your fingers. This will encourage the horse to re-balance by bringing his hind end under, rounding his back, and lightening his forehand. When the horse responds, make sure you soften your aids. The process should be for no more than three seconds depending on the balance of the horse.

   Half-halt and transitions
   Use half-halts to prepare for your transitions, letting your horse know that 'something is about to happen'. Remember that every transition counts and should always be 'without conflict'.

4. **Collection**

    When a horse works in collection he looks as though his forehand has been lifted, in reality, it is his back end that has lowered as he takes more weight on his hind in collection. As the haunches take more weight, his forehand becomes lighter.

5. **How to collect in canter**

    Once you have a feeling that there is a good amount of energy and impulsion within an established canter, start to ride some differences within the pace.
    Use a half-halt to bring the horse together slightly while ensuring that the impulsion does not die. Then ride your horse forwards to make a nice difference to the canter. You should notice a development within the canter towards some collection as the horse is achieving better balance with more weight being carried into the hind leg.

    Always remember that before you ask the horse for collection, make sure he is in front of your leg. This will ensure that you have something to collect.
    The differences within the pace will also help to engage the hind leg and aid activity within the canter which is extremely important for successful collection.

    Another good exercise to help collection of the canter is to use small circles (approximately 10m in diameter). These can help to develop the horse's balance and allows you to challenge the energy of the canter without the horse becoming too onward bound. This also helps to 'feed' the hind leg with energy without the horse running and to encourage the horse to sit within the collection.

6. **Cooling down**

    Cooling down your horse is just as important as warming up. At the end of your training session allow your horse to stretch on a light rein contact at trot, and then at walk on a loose rein to relax.

I hope this book helps you create a sense of purpose in your training and encourages you to be more creative and open for challenges. While it is good to repeat the exercises to progress, make sure you have variety in your sessions. And remember, keep a positive mind-set, give your horse time to learn and reward the effort.

Distances for Jumping and Pole work

Doubles and related distances

Horse Strides	128cms	138cms	148cms	Horses	Human paces
1	19-20ft 5.8 – 6m	21-22ft 6.4 – 6.7m	23-24ft 7 – 7.3m	24ft6"-25ft6" 7.5 – 7.8m	8
2	29-30ft 8.8 – 9m	31-32ft 9.45 – 9.75m	32-33ft 9.7 – 10m	35-36ft 10.5 – 11m	12
3	39-40ft 11.8 – 12m	41-43ft 12.5 – 13m	43-44ft 13 – 13.5m	47-48ft 14.3 – 14.5m	16
4	49-50ft 15 – 15.2m	52-53ft 15.8 – 16m	54-55ft 16.5 – 16.8m	59-60ft 18 - 18.3 -m	20
5	59-60ft 18 – 18.3m	62-63ft 18.8 – 19.2m	65-66ft 19.8 – 20.2m	70-72ft 21 – 22m	24
Bounce	9ft 2.75m	10ft 3m	10-11ft 3 – 3.3m	11-12ft 3.3 – 3.6m	3.5-4

Pole work

Trot poles	4ft 1.2m	5-6 (heel to toe)
Canter poles	9-10ft 2.7 – 3m	3 paces
Placing pole before a jump from trot	9-10ft 2.7 – 3m	3 paces
Placing pole after a jump from trot	10ft 3m	3.5 paces
Placing pole before a jump from canter	10-11ft 3.3m	3.5 paces
Placing pole after a jump from canter	10-11ft 3.3m	3.5 paces

The jumping distances are those suggested by British Showjumping for specific pony and horse classes. All distances are for guidance only and several other factors contribute such as horse/pony natural length of stride, surface, gradient, fence height and quality of canter.

Train to Progress

Repeat for Success

Tips for coaches and riders when setting up exercises

Distances

- Basic average horse stride is 12' long
- Usually, the average stride is used at the 90cms to 1m height
- Distances often must be adjusted (usually by approximately 6" for doubles and 12" for longer lines) depending on the footing, the size of the arena, grade and the level of the competitors. A distance will often ride differently when traveling toward the gate or going downhill.

Bending/Broken Lines

- A bending line is one in which there is a gradual curve from one jump to the other
- A broken line is one in which there is a distinct turn with a straight line on either side of or both sides of the turn
- When setting bending lines always take into consideration the level of the horses and riders
- The fewer the strides in a bending line the more difficult it can become.

Use of Verticals and Oxers

- The varied use of verticals and oxers can in itself create many tests and challenges for riders
- When deciding what type of fences to use, keep in mind:

    - Verticals require riders to collect and balance their horse - novice riders tend to do this by slowing down, shortening their horse's step and losing impulsion
    - Oxers tend to make riders become very loose in the air, making it difficult to organise for the next jump

Combinations

- Vertical to oxer – simple and easy for novice / intermediate riders
- Oxer to vertical – tests a rider's ability to land in balance after the oxer and organize for the vertical coming out
- Vertical to vertical – less difficult, especially when set on a shorter distance; when set on a longer distance it requires riders to maintain a forward pace while still needing to be balanced and organised
- Oxer to oxer – really makes a rider maintain forward pace and impulsion while being in control of their upper body and using their seat and legs for support

Train to Progress

Repeat for Success

Keys for Diagrams

· · · · · · · · · · · · · · ·   **Trot**

- - - - - - - - - - - - -   **Canter**

●   Training Cone

■   Training Block

↕   Upright Jump

↕   Parallel Jump/Oxer

—   Trotting Pole

Guide for exercise difficulty

● Easy - Suitable for young horses, and riders focussing on basic training.

● Moderate – For horses/riders competent in working in rhythm and balance.

● Challenging – For horses/riders well established in all six 'scales of training.'

Train to Progress

Repeat for Success

Exercise 1 - Straightness

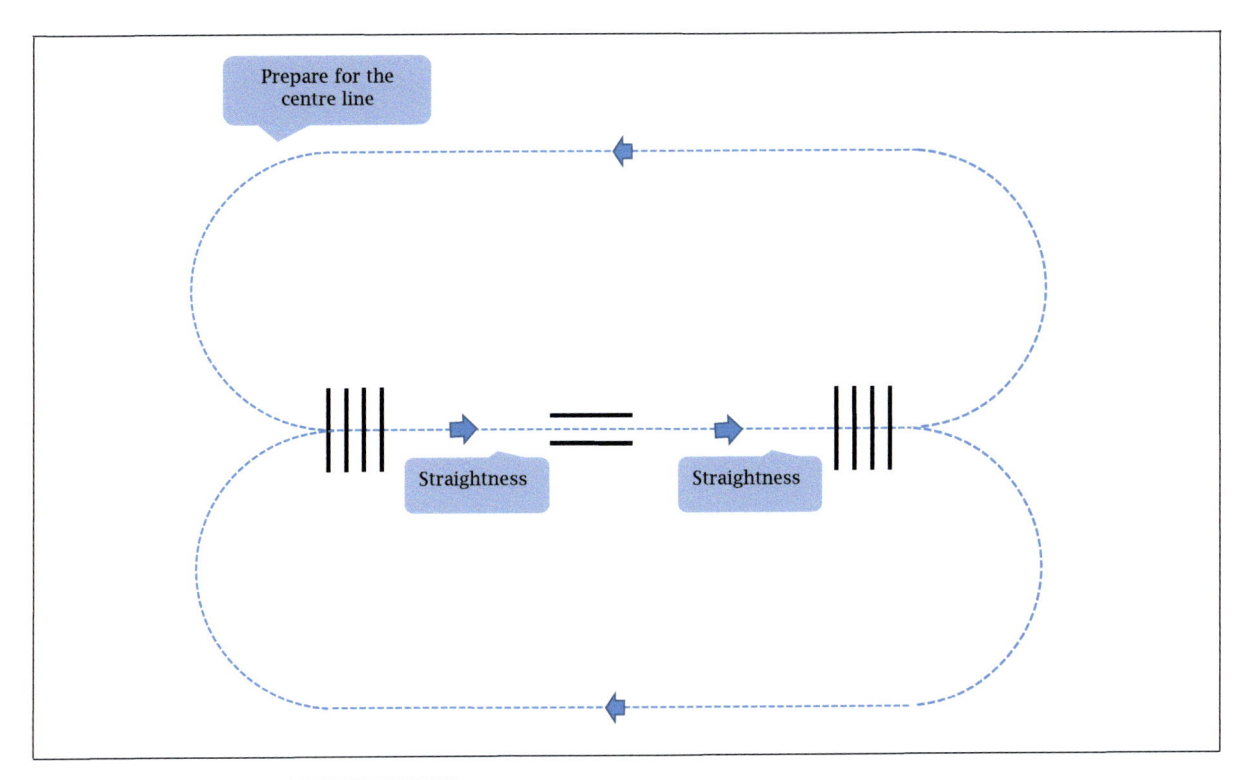

Start on either rein in a forward trot with a good rhythm. Turn either way down the centre line, focussing on straightness, and alternate which direction you turn at the other end of the arena.

The rider should be aware of sitting straight and tall with even weight in both stirrups to help the horse with straightness.

The rider must then collect the horse with a half-halt before each turn.

Aims:
- ✓ To be straight down the centre line to both sets of poles
- ✓ To maintain the rhythm and balance between the poles
- ✓ To change the bend smoothly
- ✓ To keep the bend consistent on the turns

Coach's Tips:
- Think about your rider position, sit tall, have a secure lower leg with the heel lower than the toe
- Use the half-halt to collect and prepare for the change of bend before the turn
- Look early on the turns to find the straight line

Progression:
When you feel competent, move on to exercise 1a.

Exercise 1a – Straightness

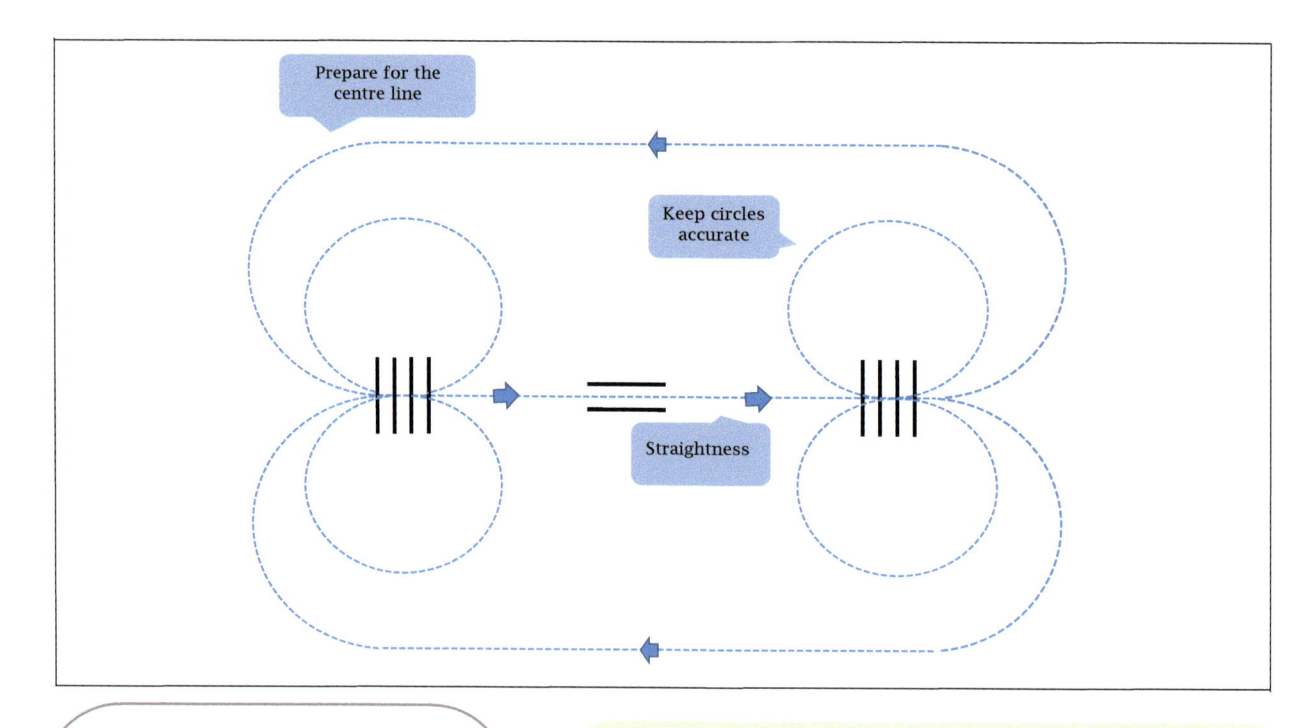

Diagram labels: Prepare for the centre line; Keep circles accurate; Straightness

Start on either rein in a forward trot with a good rhythm. Turn either way down the centre line focussing on straightness. If you have turned right down the centre line, then after the poles make a small circle left returning to the poles again. Stay straight down the centre line over the next set of poles and make a small circle right, returning back to the poles again. Repeat and alternate the direction of the circles.

The rider must collect the horse with a half-halt before each turn and circle.

Aims:
- ✓ To be straight down the centre line to both sets of poles
- ✓ To maintain the rhythm and balance throughout
- ✓ To be accurate in the size of the circles
- ✓ To check the horse is equally supple on both reins

Coach's Tips:
- Look early on the turns to find the straight line
- The rider must be accurate on the turns, both onto and away from the centre line
- Use the half-halt to collect and prepare for both the turns and the circles

Progression:
When you feel competent, move on to exercise 1b.

Exercise 1b – Straightness

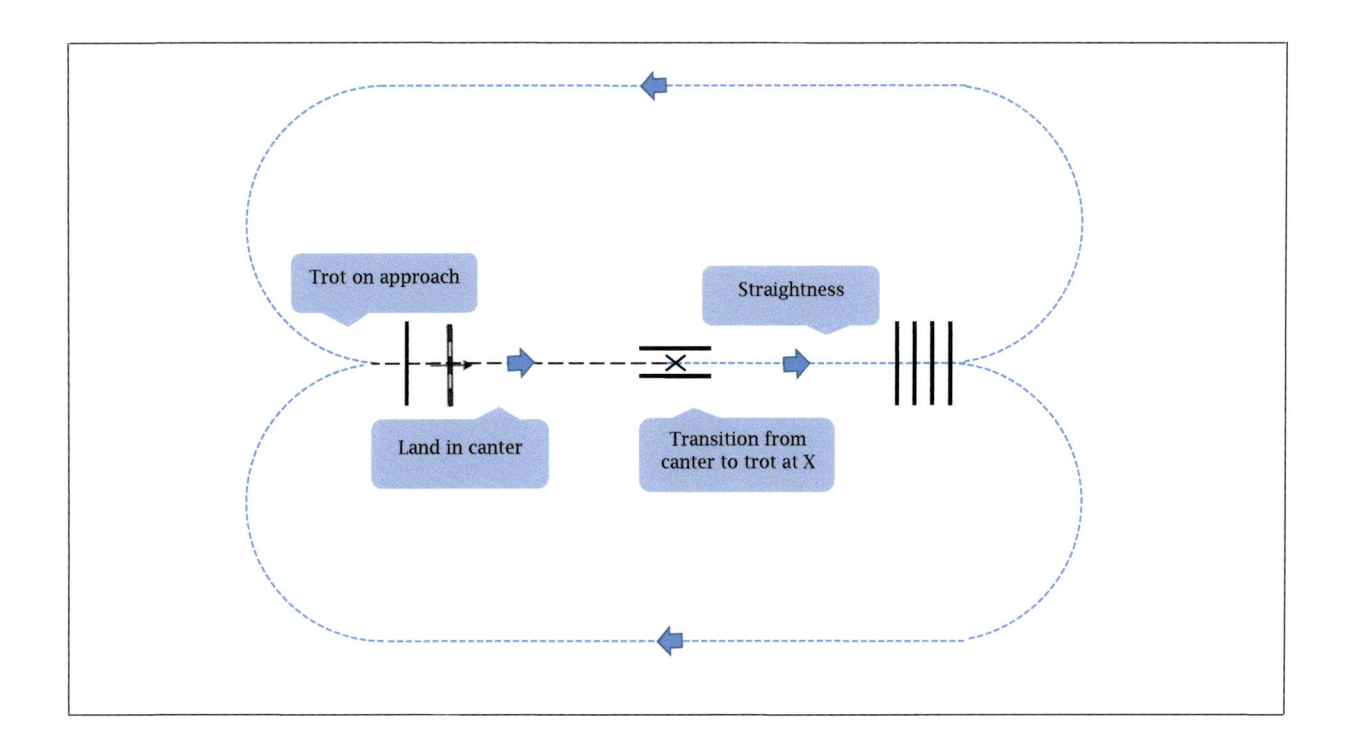

Diagram labels: Trot on approach; Straightness; Land in canter; Transition from canter to trot at X

Start on either rein in a forward trot with a good rhythm. Turn either way down the centre line focussing on straightness. Jump the small jump and land in canter. Between the two poles at X make a transition to trot and stay straight to the trotting poles.

The rider should be aware of sitting central with even weight in both stirrups to help maintain straightness. Alternate from each direction. Repeat until executed smoothly.

Aims:
- ✓ To be straight down the centre line
- ✓ To make a smooth transition to trot after the jump
- ✓ To increase rider/horse communication
- ✓ To change the bend smoothly

Coach's Tips:
- The rider must be accurate on the turns, both onto and away from the centre line
- Use the half-halt to collect and prepare for the transition from canter to trot
- Rider aids should never be hard or aggressive, repeat and give your horse time to learn

Exercise 2 - Straightness and transitions

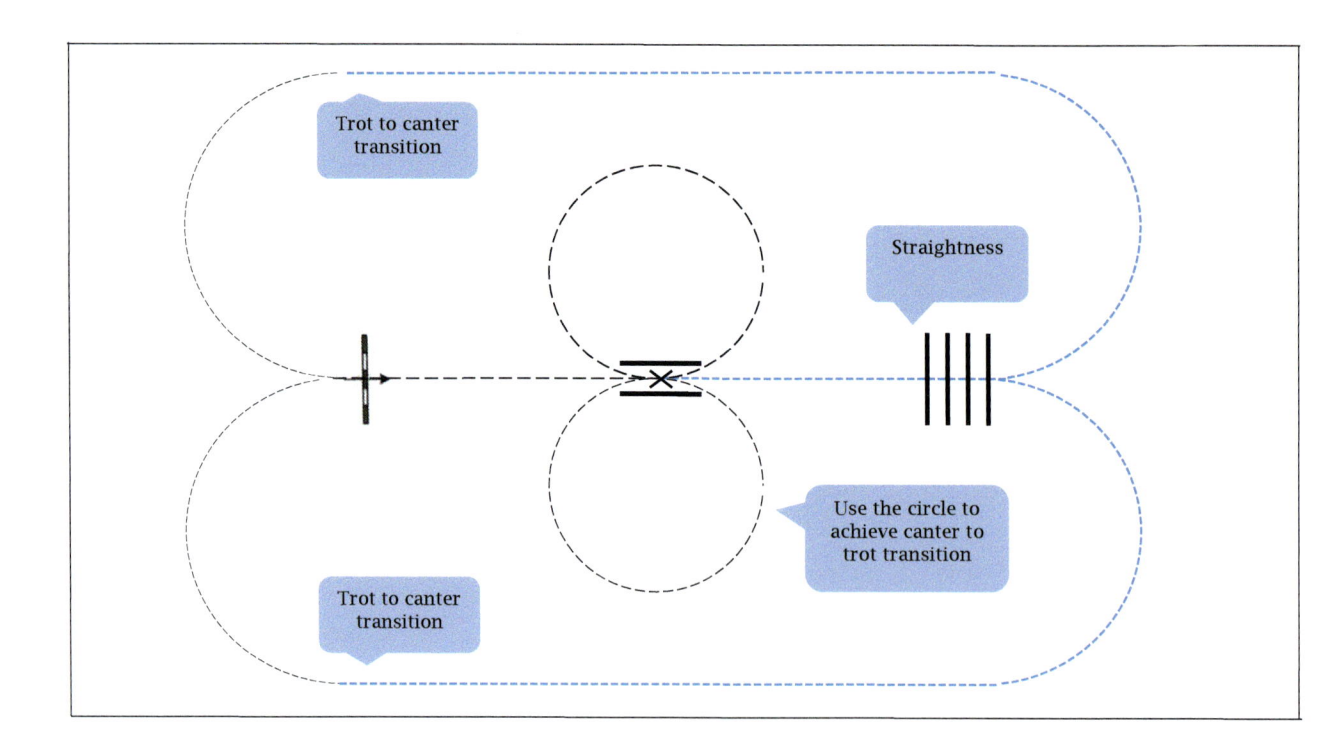

Diagram labels:
- Trot to canter transition
- Straightness
- Use the circle to achieve canter to trot transition
- Trot to canter transition

Start on either rein in a collected canter with a good rhythm. Turn either way down the centre line focussing on straightness.

Jump the small jump from canter. Between the two poles at X make a transition to trot and stay straight to the trotting poles.
Use the small circles to achieve a smooth transition if necessary.

Remember to change canter lead when needed.

Aims:
- ✓ To be straight down the centre line
- ✓ To make a smooth transition to trot after the jump
- ✓ To increase rider/horse communication
- ✓ To change the bend smoothly

Coach's Tips:
- The rider must be accurate on the turns, both onto and away from the centre line
- Use the half-halt to collect and prepare for the transition from canter to trot
- Check that you are sat in balance, and in the centre of your saddle

Progression:
Move on to exercise 2a when transitions are smooth and relaxed.

Exercise 2a - Straightness in Canter

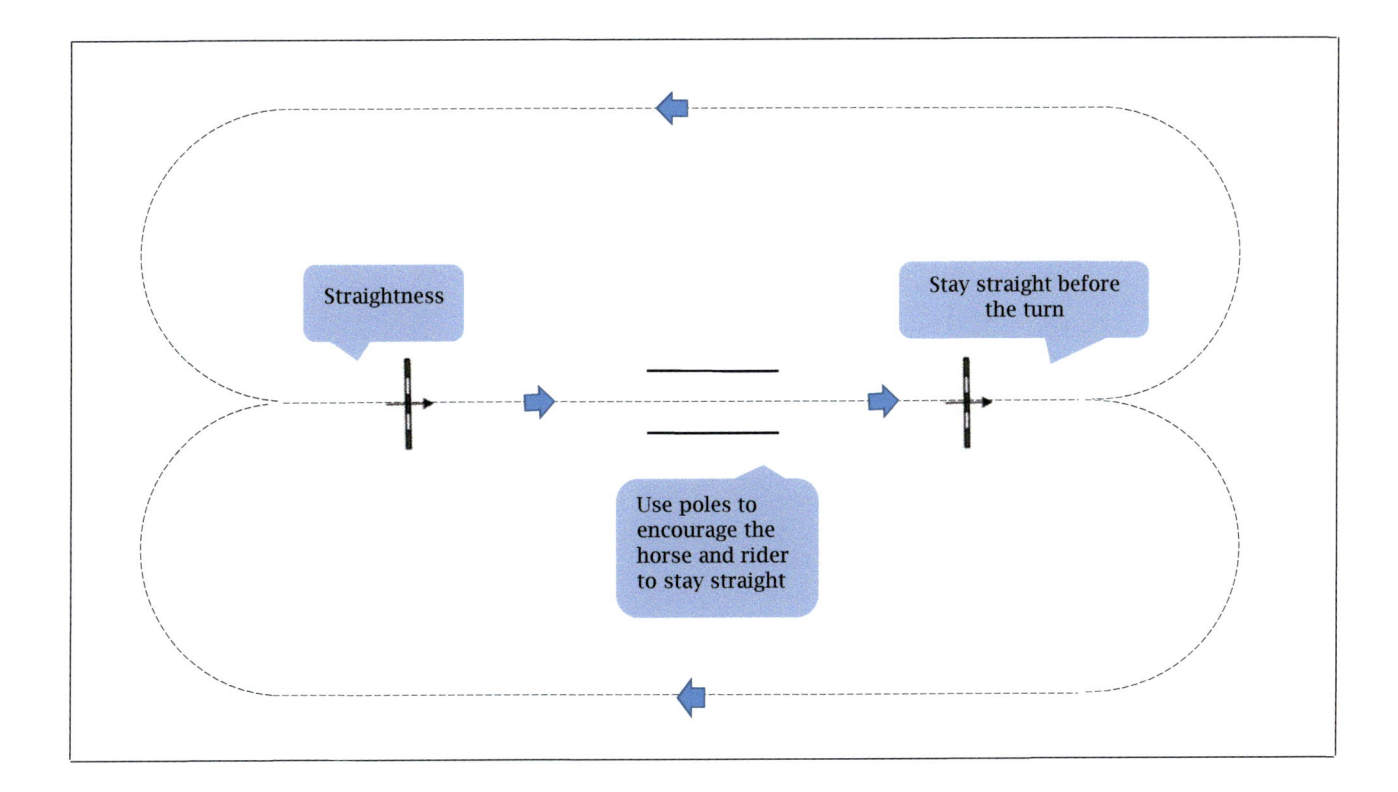

Diagram labels:
- Straightness
- Stay straight before the turn
- Use poles to encourage the horse and rider to stay straight

Place two jumps on the straight line with a distance of at least 5 or 6 horse strides between. Start on either rein in a collected canter with a good rhythm. Turn either way down the centre line, focussing on straightness, and alternate which direction you turn at the other end of the arena. The rider should be aware of sitting straight and tall with even weight in both stirrups to help the horse with straightness, and collect the horse with a half-halt before each turn.

Remember to change canter lead when necessary.

Aims:
- To be straight down the centre line to both poles
- To maintain the rhythm between the poles
- To keep central to the poles
- To keep the bend consistent on the turns

Coach's Tips:
- Look early on the turns to find the straight line
- The rider must be accurate on the turns, both onto and away from the centre line
- Use the half-halt to collect and prepare for the change of bend

Progression:
Increase the difficulty by changing the poles into two small jumps.
Have the jumps on a distance of at least 5 horse strides to allow for adaptability.

Exercise 2b – Straightness and circles

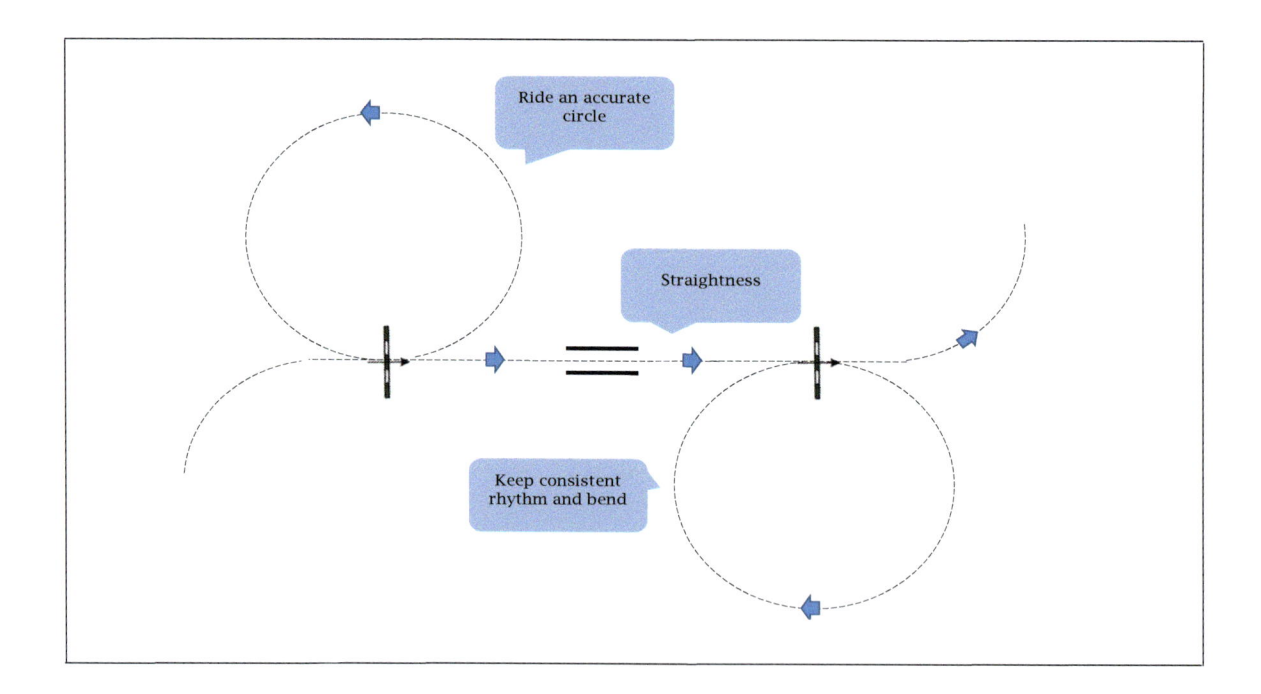

Diagram labels: Ride an accurate circle; Straightness; Keep consistent rhythm and bend

Start on the right rein in a collected canter with a good rhythm. Turn down the centre line focussing on straightness.

Jump the small jump from canter then circle left and jump the jump again.

Continue straight down the centre line and jump the next jump, circling to the right before jumping the jump again. Turn left at the end of the arena.

Remember to correct the lead on landing if necessary.

Aims:
- ✓ To be straight down the centre line
- ✓ To ride accurate circles
- ✓ To increase rider/horse communication
- ✓ To encourage a collected canter
- ✓ To stop the horse anticipating the direction

Coach's Tips:
- The rider must be accurate on the circles
- Use the circles to increase collection
- Rider must anticipate the horse falling in or out on the circle

Progression:
Use four circles to alternate the direction.
Work on influencing the horse to land on the correct lead.

Exercise 2c - Straightness and diagonal lines

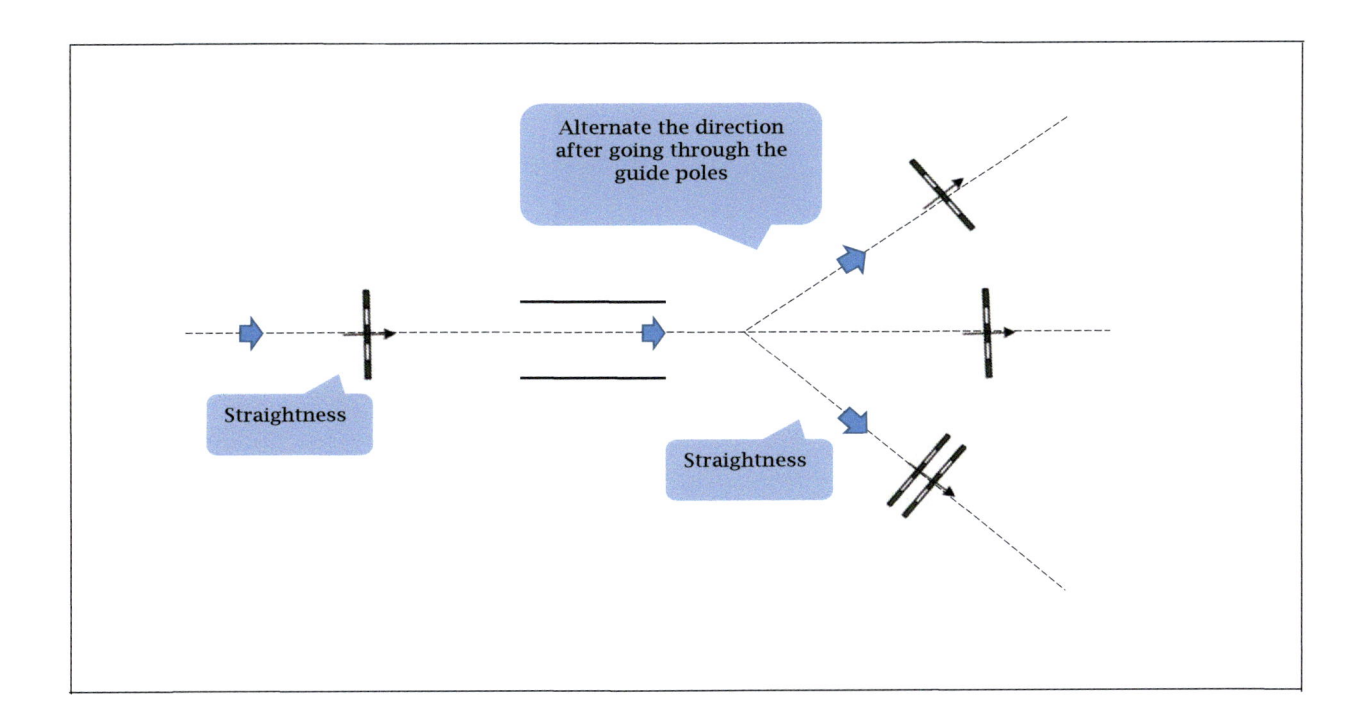

Diagram labels:
- Alternate the direction after going through the guide poles
- Straightness
- Straightness

Add two more jumps on the diagonal to exercise 2b.
Start on either rein in a collected canter with good rhythm. Turn either way down the centre line focussing on straightness to the two jumps.
Next time you turn down the centre decide which of the jumps you are going to jump after going through the guide poles.

Keep alternating the direction making sure you give the horse clear and early instructions.

Aims:
- ✓ To be straight down the centre line
- ✓ To ride accurate lines
- ✓ To increase rider/horse communication
- ✓ To stop the horse anticipating the direction

Coach's Tips:
- The rider must be accurate on the lines
- The rider must anticipate the horse falling in or out on the line
- The rider needs to stay central with even weight in both stirrups so that the turns are ridden in balance

Progression:
Move on to exercise 2d when you feel relaxed and confident with your horse's progress.

Exercise 2d – Turning back to straight lines

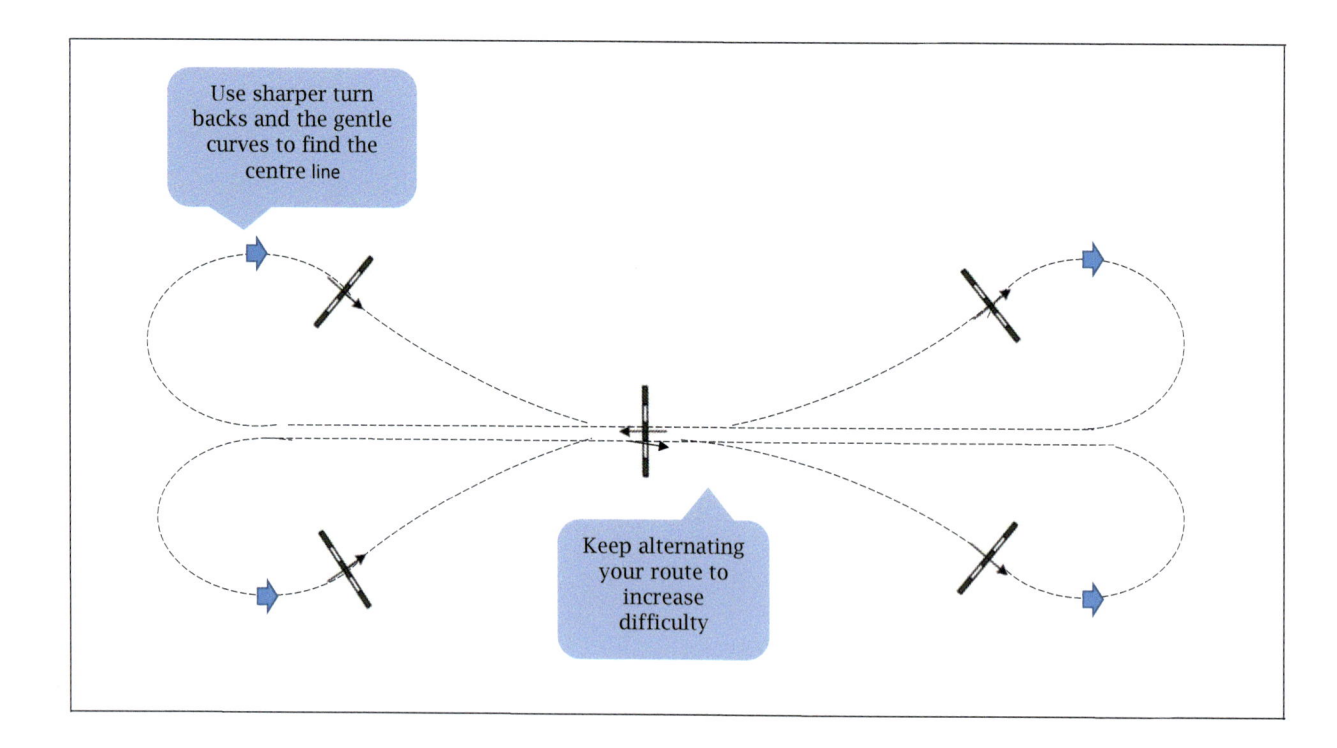

Use sharper turn backs and the gentle curves to find the centre line

Keep alternating your route to increase difficulty

Start on either rein in a collected canter with a good rhythm. Turn either way down the centre line, focussing on straightness, to the central jump. Prior to completing the central jump decide which direction you will turn to the next jump.

Then turn back down the centre line complete the central jump and again complete a second jump in the chosen direction. Keep alternating the direction making sure you give the horse clear and early instructions.

Aims:

- ✓ To improve collection and balance through the turns
- ✓ To improve rider/horse communication
- ✓ To see if the horse is equally supple when turning both directions

Coach's tips:

- Make sure the horse does not fall out through the shoulder on the turn back
- Be accurate on the straightness to the jump as well as the turns
- Use the half-halt to prepare the horse for the turn

Exercise 3 - Riding accurate diagonal lines

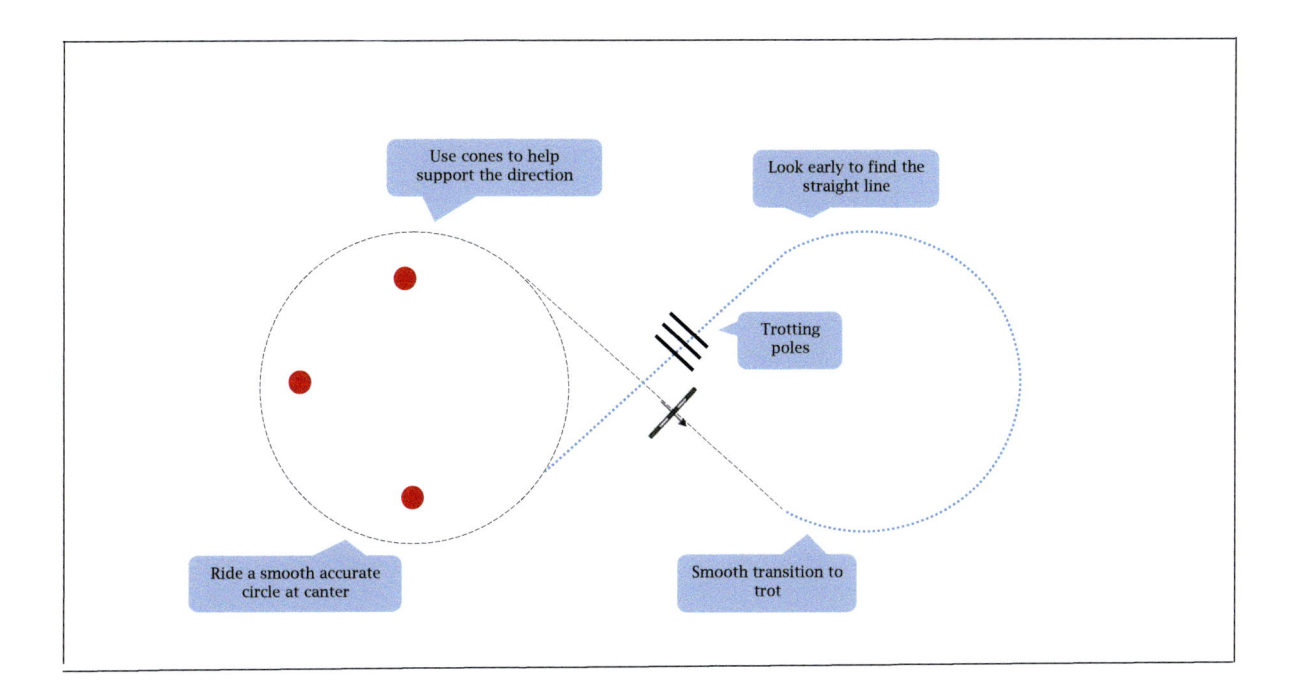

Use cones to help support the direction

Look early to find the straight line

Trotting poles

Ride a smooth accurate circle at canter

Smooth transition to trot

Start in canter on a circle around the cones before continuing straight across the diagonal to a small jump.

Canter away straight and make a transition to trot before make a smooth turn back across the diagonal to the trotting poles.

Finish by cantering another circle around the cones.

Aims:
- ✓ To improve accurate turns in preparation for diagonal lines
- ✓ To increase rider/horse communication
- ✓ To improve transitions

Coach's tips:
- The rider needs to focus ahead giving the horse clear instructions
- Collect the horse with half-halts before each transition
- Stay relaxed and give the horse time to learn

Progression:
Change the trotting poles into a small jump and complete the figure of 8 in canter as shown in exercise 3a.

Exercise 3a - Riding accurate diagonal lines

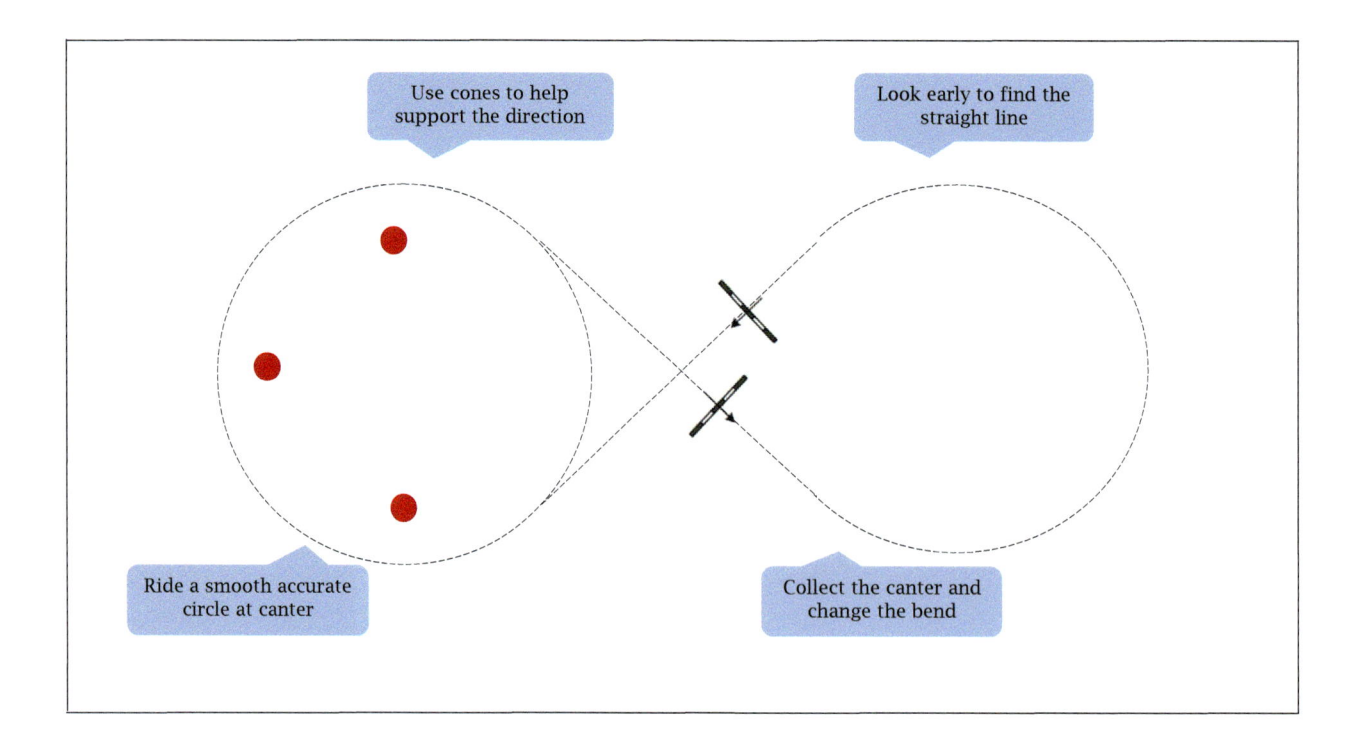

Diagram callouts:
- Use cones to help support the direction
- Look early to find the straight line
- Ride a smooth accurate circle at canter
- Collect the canter and change the bend

Canter a circle on the right rein around the cones. When balanced with a good rhythm continue across the diagonal to the small jump.

Stay straight on landing, correcting the lead, if necessary, going into the bend. Complete the figure of 8 by jumping the small jump across the other diagonal.

Canter a circle around the cones to balance the horse to finish.

Aims:
- ✓ To improve straightness across the diagonal
- ✓ To check that the horse is equally supple turning in both directions
- ✓ To increase collection and balance after the jump

Coach's Tips:
- Be ready to prevent the horse from falling in or out on the turns
- Leaving the circle, or turn, too early will cause the horse to be unbalanced and crooked across the diagonal to the jump

Progression:
To increase difficulty, continue to exercise 3b.

Exercise 3b - Riding accurate diagonal lines and turns

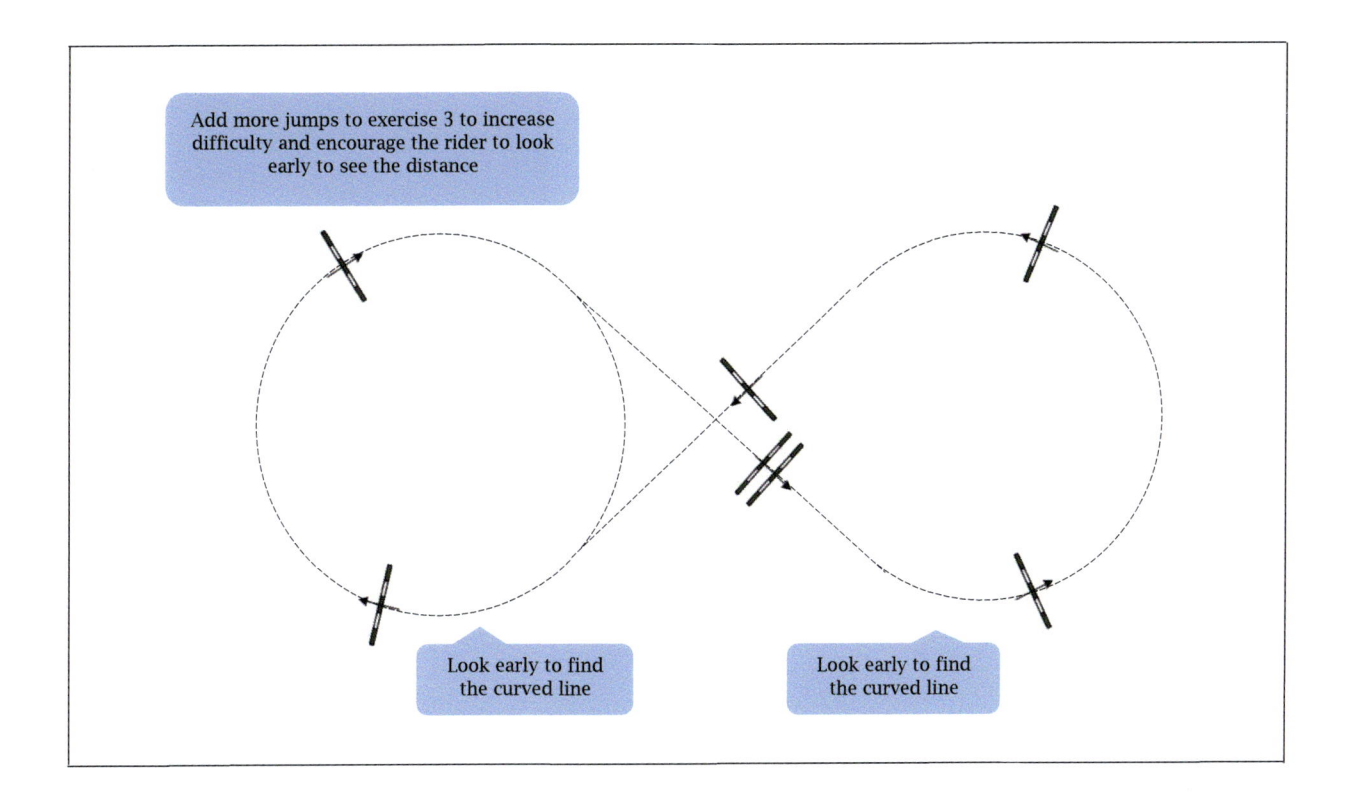

Add more jumps to exercise 3 to increase difficulty and encourage the rider to look early to see the distance

Look early to find the curved line

Look early to find the curved line

Progress from exercise 3a by adding two more small jumps on each of the turns to increase the difficulty.

Keep the jumps small to enable the rider to focus on the accuracy of the bends and the straightness across the diagonal.

Aims:

- ✓ To increase the focus from both the rider and the horse
- ✓ To encourage the rider to plan ahead and think quickly
- ✓ To improve rider/horse communication

Coach's tips:

- Keep your body balance central and look early to the next jump to find the line and the distance
- Don't let yourself feel rushed, canter an occasional circle without the jumps to rebalance if necessary

Exercise 4 – Lengthening and shortening strides

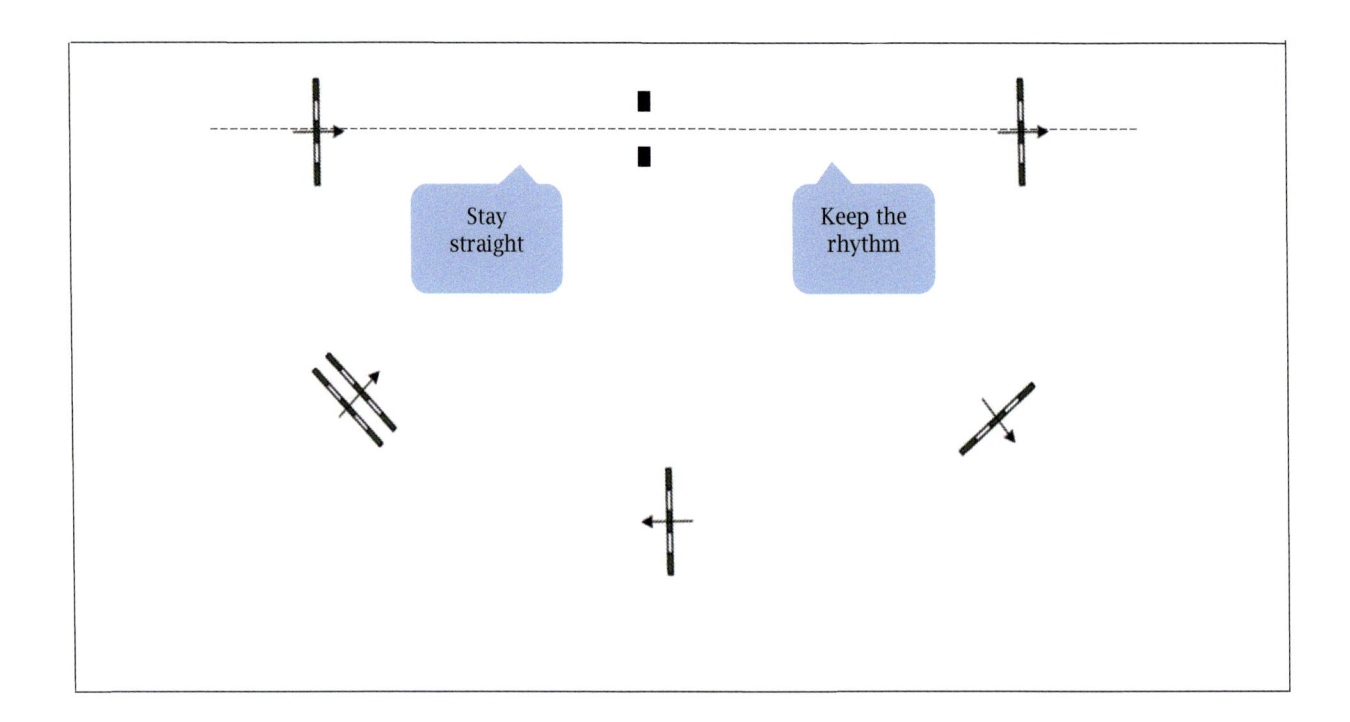

Place two poles on a straight line down the long side of the arena. These should be at least 5 or 6 horse strides apart to allow for adaptability. Start in canter on the right rein and ride a straight line over both poles. Count how many strides your horse takes in natural canter strides. Repeat adding an extra stride between the two poles by shortening the length of canter stride. Use cones/blocks to help maintain straightness. Repeat the exercise on the opposite rein.

Aims:
- ✓ To improve variation in length of canter stride by alternating the number of strides
- ✓ To assess the rhythm and balance of the horse's canter stride
- ✓ To increase rider/horse communication

Coach's tips:
- The rider should maintain rhythm when shortening and lengthening, and not slow down or quicken in pace
- Keep even weight in both stirrups and even contact down both reins to encourage the horse to stay straight

Progression:
Replace the poles with two small jumps when the horse feels more adaptable in the canter.

Exercise 4a - Straightness and circles

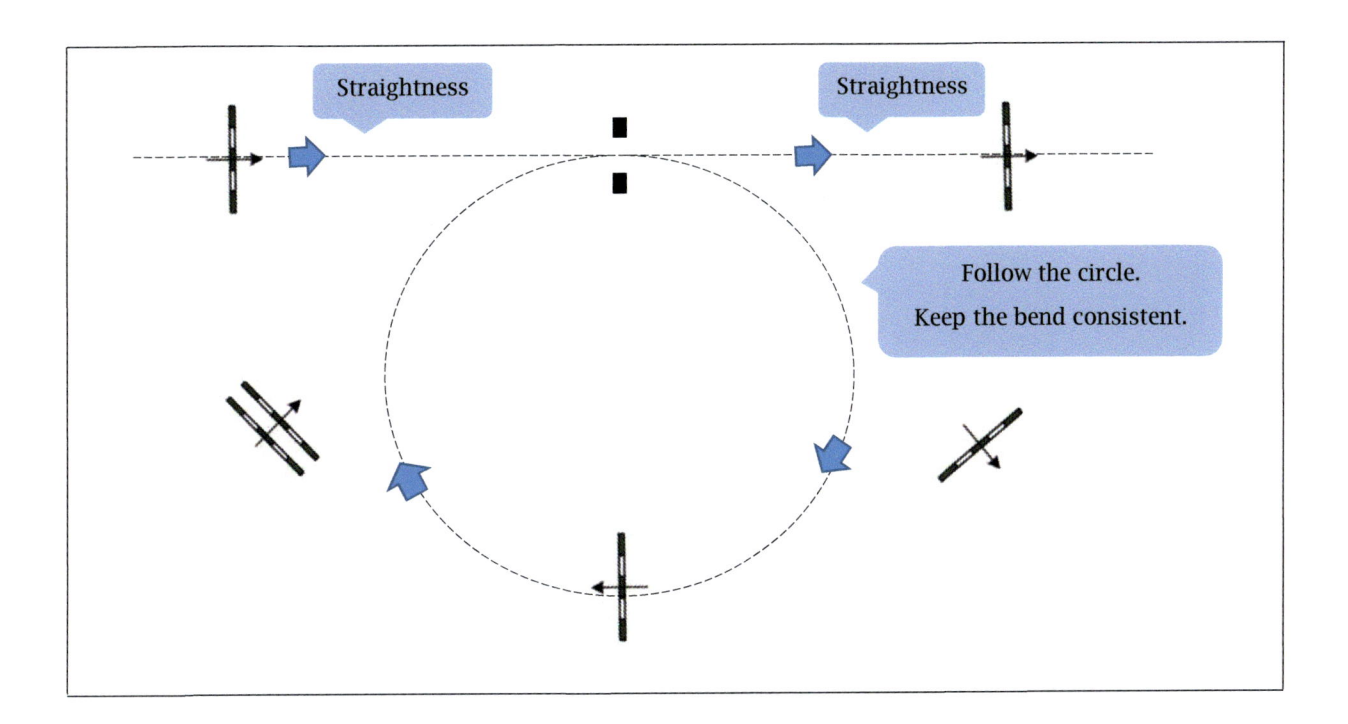

(Diagram: A rectangular arena showing a straight dashed line across the top with two jumps marked "Straightness" and directional arrows. A dashed circle in the middle incorporates a small jump, with label "Follow the circle. Keep the bend consistent." Additional jumps are placed outside the circle.)

Progress from exercise 4. Place two jumps on the straight line with a distance of at least 5 or 6 horse strides between, then place another small jump on a circle.

Ride in canter to the first jump on the straight line, then start a circle when going through the cones incorporating the small jump. Return back through the cones and continue on the straight line to the final jump.

Repeat from the opposite direction.

Aims:

- ✓ To increase rider/horse communication
- ✓ To encourage the rider to plan ahead
- ✓ To maintain rhythm and balance both on the straight line and the circle
- ✓ To refrain the horse from rushing on the straight line

Coach's tips:

- Prepare the horse for the circle with a half-halt before the cones
- Look early for the circle and jump
- The rider's shoulders and hips should be parallel to each jump to be in balance

Progression:
Move on to exercise 4b to increase difficulty.

Exercise 4b - Straightness, circles and diagonals

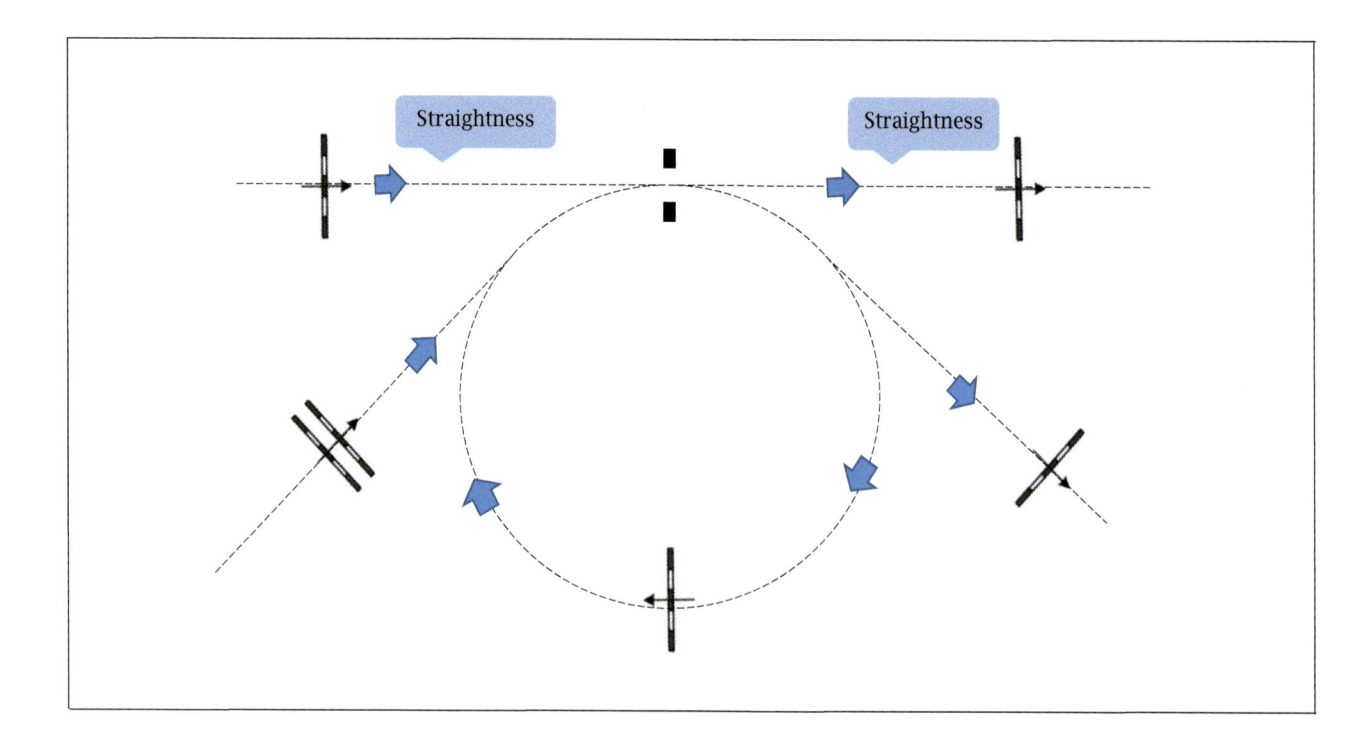

Progress from exercise 4b by adding diagonal lines to the exercise.

This can be ridden from the straight line, on to the jump on the circle, through the cones and then across the diagonal.

Increase difficulty by starting on the diagonal, followed by the jump on the circle, finishing with the opposite diagonal. Repeat from the opposite direction.

Aims:

- ✓ To encourage the rider to look ahead and think quickly
- ✓ To improve rider/horse communication
- ✓ To stop the horse from anticipating the jump and direction

Coach's tips:

- Look early to the jump and give clear directions
- Don't allow yourself to feel rushed
- Return to an easy line if the horse begins to feel tense

Progression:
Move on to exercise 4c to further establish your turns and straightness.

Exercise 4c - Straightness and accurate turns

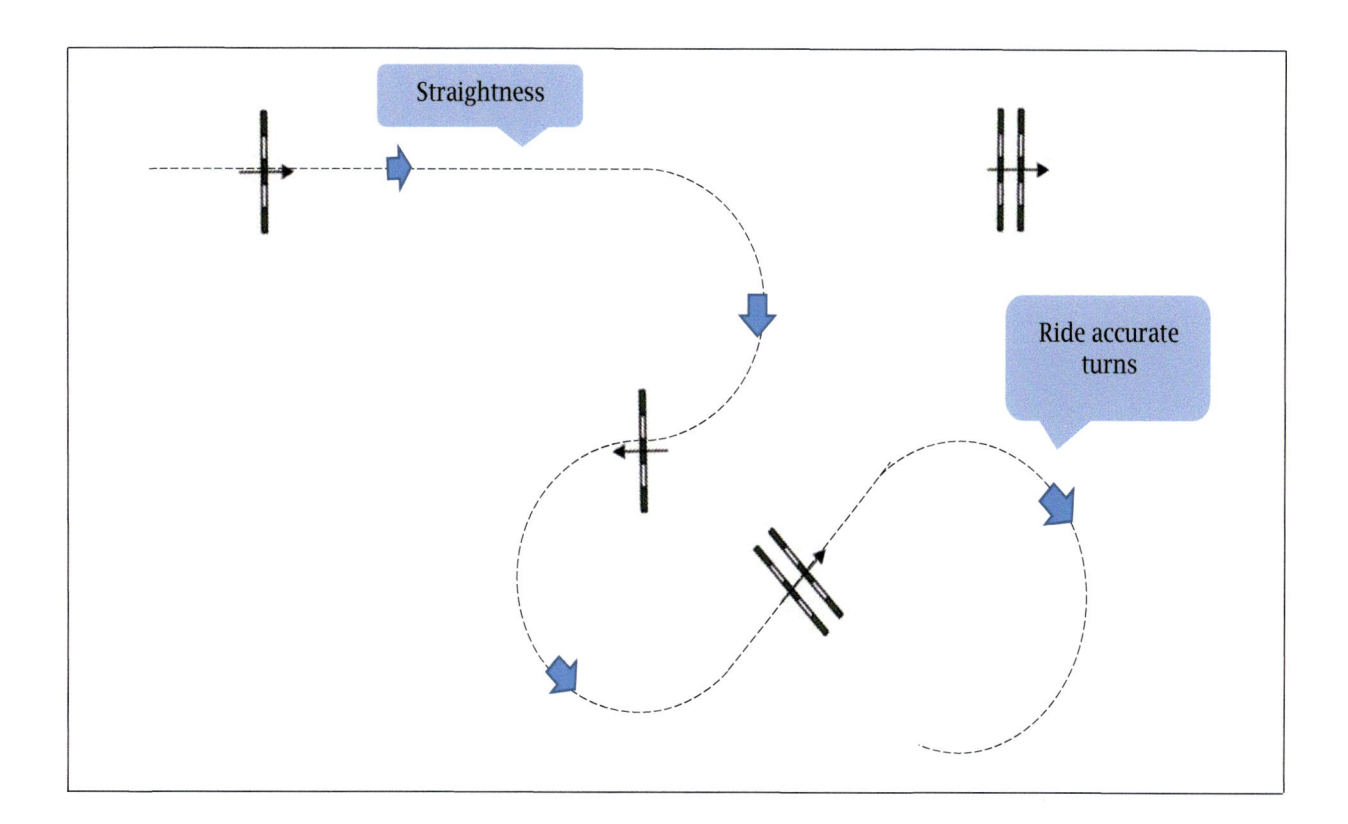

Diagram labels: Straightness; Ride accurate turns

Start in canter on the right rein to the jump staying straight on landing.

Plan a smooth, accurate turn back to the right making sure you are straight to the jump. Make another smooth, accurate turn back to the left to the next jump and turn back to the right to finish.

Repeat from the other direction.

Aims:

- ✓ To plan ahead and ride accurate turns
- ✓ To maintain balance and rhythm on the turns
- ✓ To improve focus from the horse
- ✓ To check the horse is equally supple turning from both directions

Coach's tips:

- The rider's hips and shoulders should be parallel to the jumps to ensure straightness and balance
- Look early to the jump to ride accurate turns

Exercise 5 - Riding accurate lines

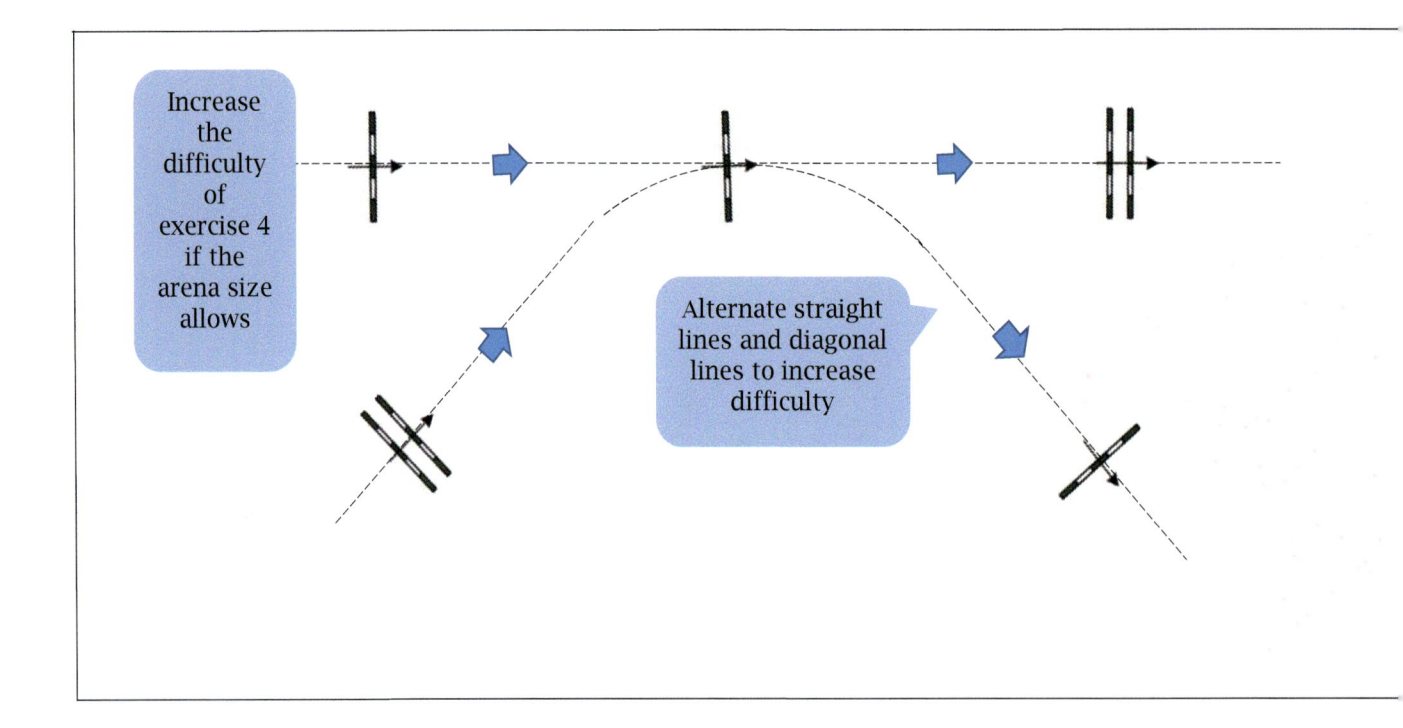

Increase the difficulty of exercise 4 if the arena size allows

Alternate straight lines and diagonal lines to increase difficulty

If arena size allows, continue from exercise 4 with three jumps on a straight line 4 or 5 horse strides apart.

This exercise can be ridden from the straight line to the diagonal line, or from diagonal to diagonal, to increase the difficulty.

Make sure you ride the exercise in both directions.

Aims:
- ✓ To encourage forward planning from the rider
- ✓ To increase accuracy when riding lines
- ✓ To improve rider/horse communication

Coach's tips:
- Look early to find your line
- Be aware of the horse anticipating the turns and falling in
- Be patient and return to an easier line if the horse becomes tense

Progression:
Move on to exercise 5a when you feel ready.

Exercise 5a - Riding accurate lines

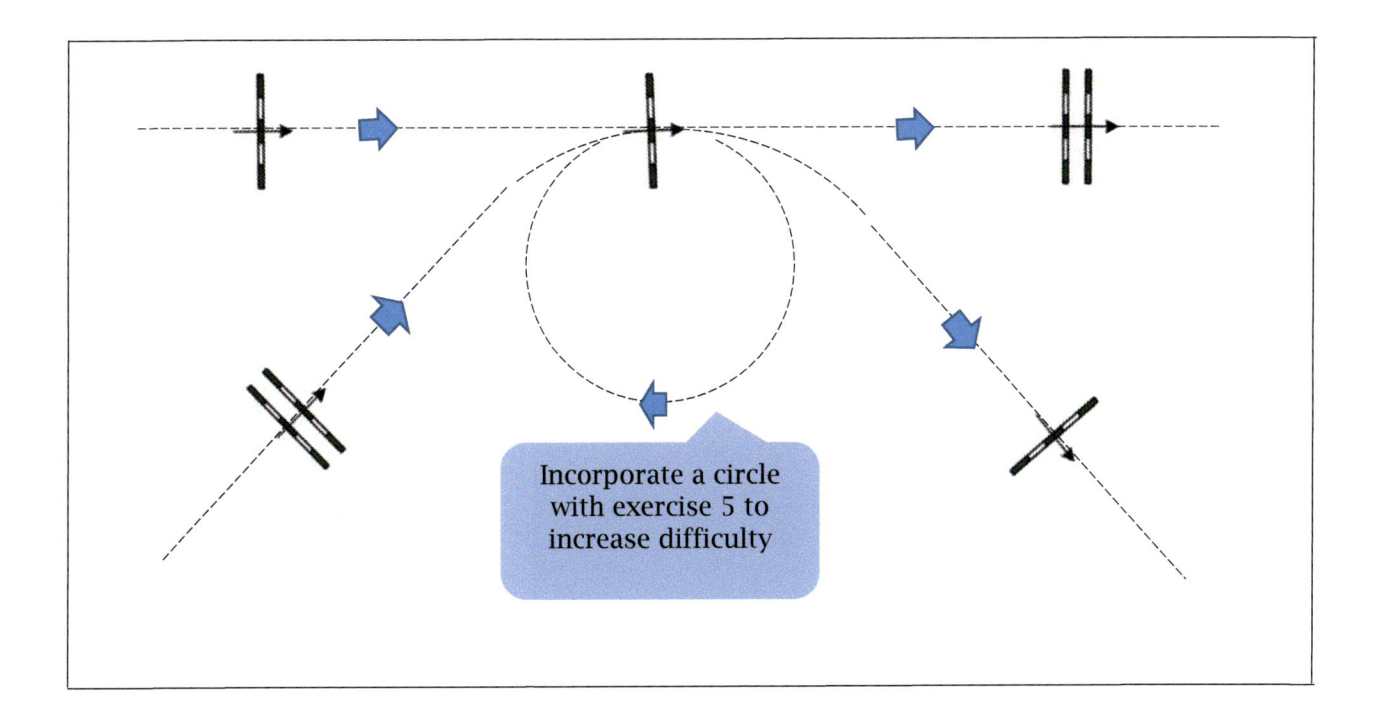

Incorporate a circle with exercise 5 to increase difficulty

Increase the difficulty of exercise 5 by adding a circle after the middle jump on the straight line.

You can alternate between going straight or across the diagonal after completing the circle, or by riding from the diagonal, to the circle, to the diagonal.

Alternate the direction of the exercise to keep your work even.

Aims:
- ✓ To use the circle to keep the horse's attention and not anticipate the jump
- ✓ To encourage the rider to plan ahead
- ✓ To improve rider/horse communication

Coach's tips
- Alternate between using the circle sometimes and not others to keep the horse listening
- Be accurate with your lines and keep 'on the boil'

Progression:
For increase of rider focus move on to exercise 5b.

Exercise 5b - Riding accurate lines

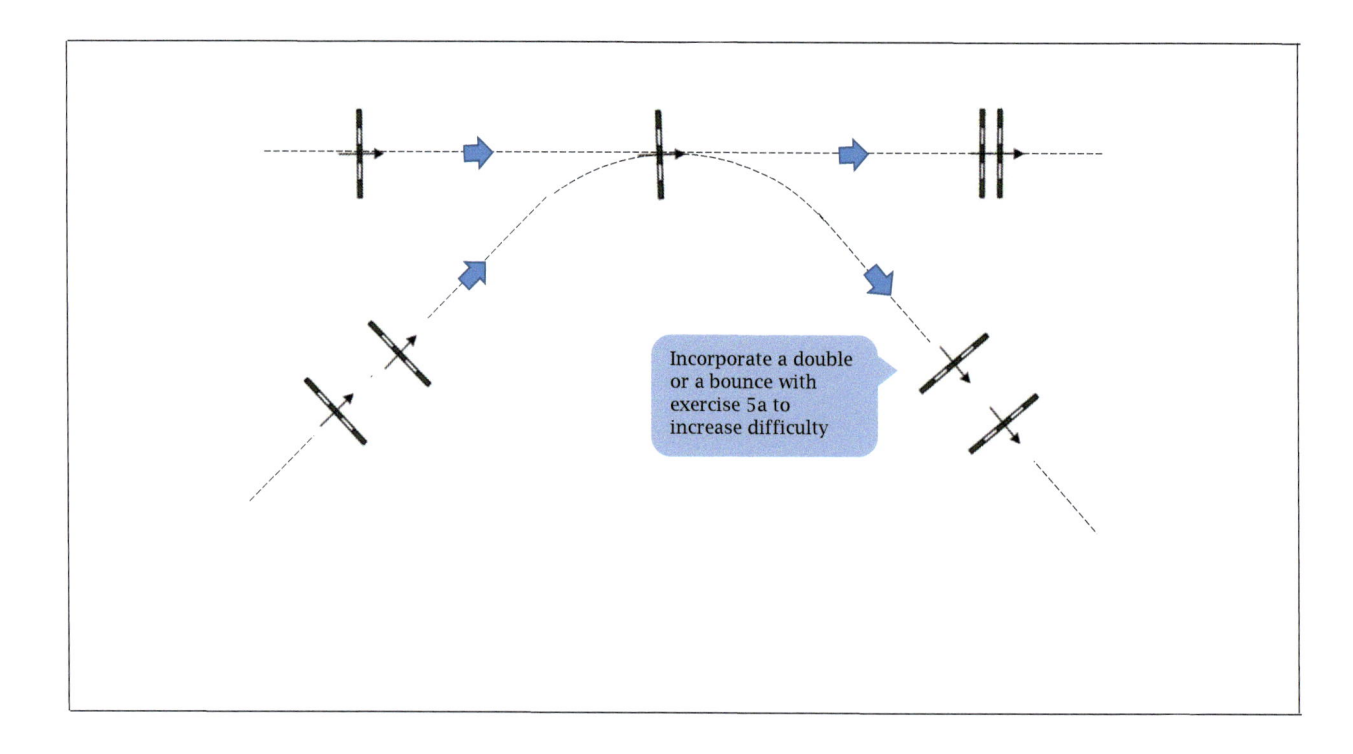

Incorporate a double or a bounce with exercise 5a to increase difficulty

To increase the difficulty of exercise 5a, incorporate either two doubles or two bounces (check the distances table when setting up).

This exercise further increases the importance of straightness on both the straight lines and the diagonals.

Remember to ride this exercise in both directions.

Aims:

- ✓ To further highlight the importance of straightness
- ✓ To increase forward planning from the rider
- ✓ To improve accuracy of lines

Coach's tips:

- If your horse is unaccustomed to bounces either ride to these on their own first or use a one stride double
- Alternate between straight lines and diagonal lines to encourage the horse to listen

Exercise 6 – Increasing suppleness

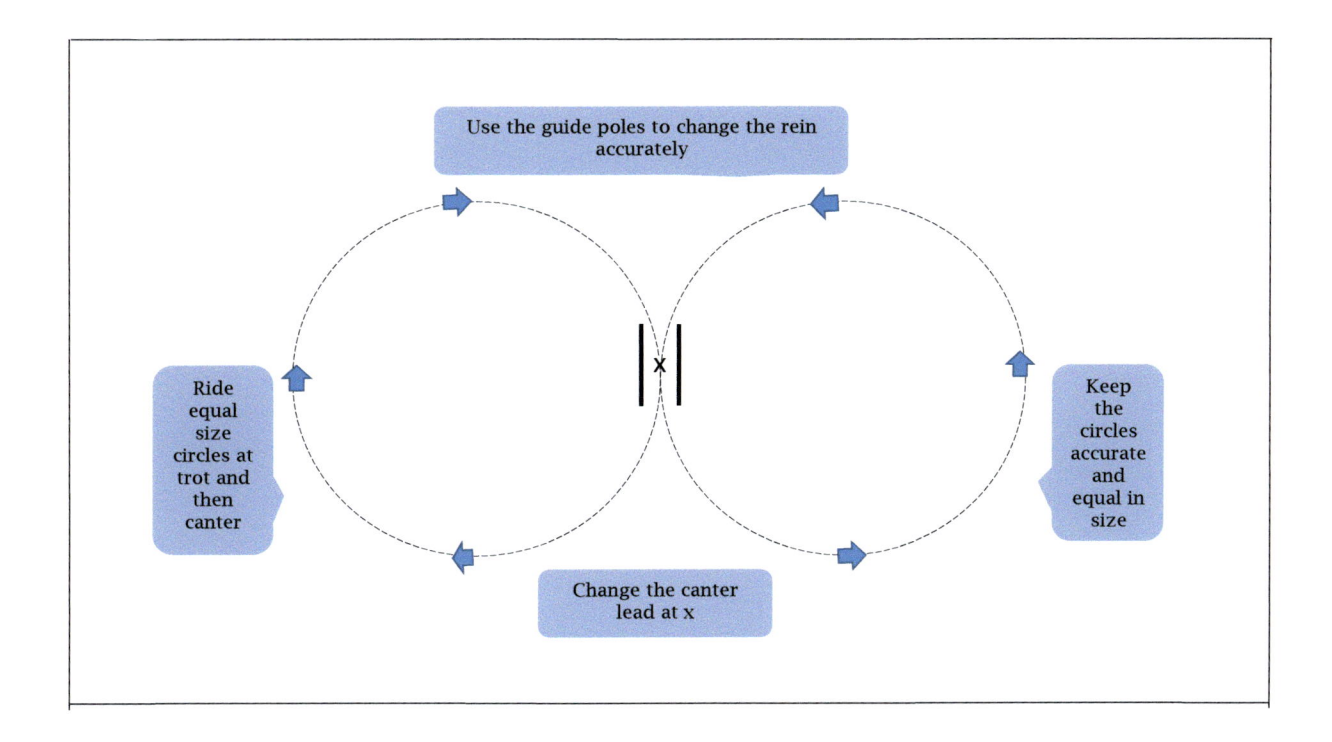

Diagram labels:
- Use the guide poles to change the rein accurately
- Ride equal size circles at trot and then canter
- Keep the circles accurate and equal in size
- Change the canter lead at x

Place two poles parallel across the centre line. Ride a figure of eight at trot, focusing on the change of rein at X.

When the horse is feeling relaxed continue with the exercise in canter.

Remember to change the lead and the bend between the poles.

Aims:
- ✓ To learn if your horse is equally supple on both reins
- ✓ To ride accurate circles of equal size
- ✓ To keep a consistent bend through the horse's body
- ✓ To feel if the horse is falling in or out on the circle

Coach's tips:
- Make sure you use a half-halt to collect your horse before x
- Remember to be straight for a couple of strides before changing the bend

Progression:
Move on to exercise 6a when your horse feels supple and relaxed.

Exercise 6a – Suppleness and variation in canter strides

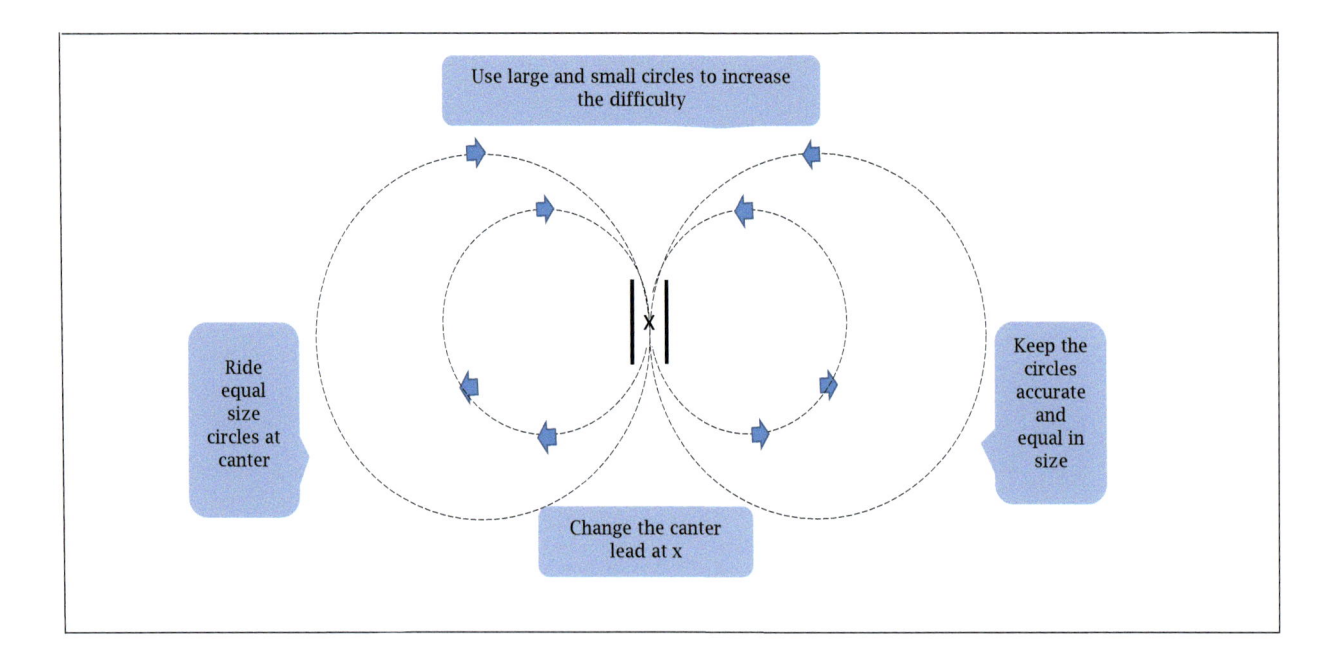

Diagram labels:
- Use large and small circles to increase the difficulty
- Ride equal size circles at canter
- Keep the circles accurate and equal in size
- Change the canter lead at x

Increase the difficulty of exercise 6 by cantering a figure of 8, using the bigger circles first.

When the horse is relaxed and focussed start incorporating the smaller figure of 8 to increase difficulty.

Use trot transitions or flying changes at x depending on the horse's experience.

Remember to repeat the exercise on both reins.

Aims:
- To ride accurate circles of different sizes
- To increase collection of the canter on the smaller circles
- To have appropriate bend for the size of the circle

Coach's tips:
- The rider must feel if the horse is falling in or out on the circles and take action
- Keep the horse interested by varying the canter (e.g. bigger canter on the larger circle, more collection on the smaller circle)

Progression:
Move on to exercise 6b when you feel ready.

Exercise 6b – Increasing Suppleness and collection

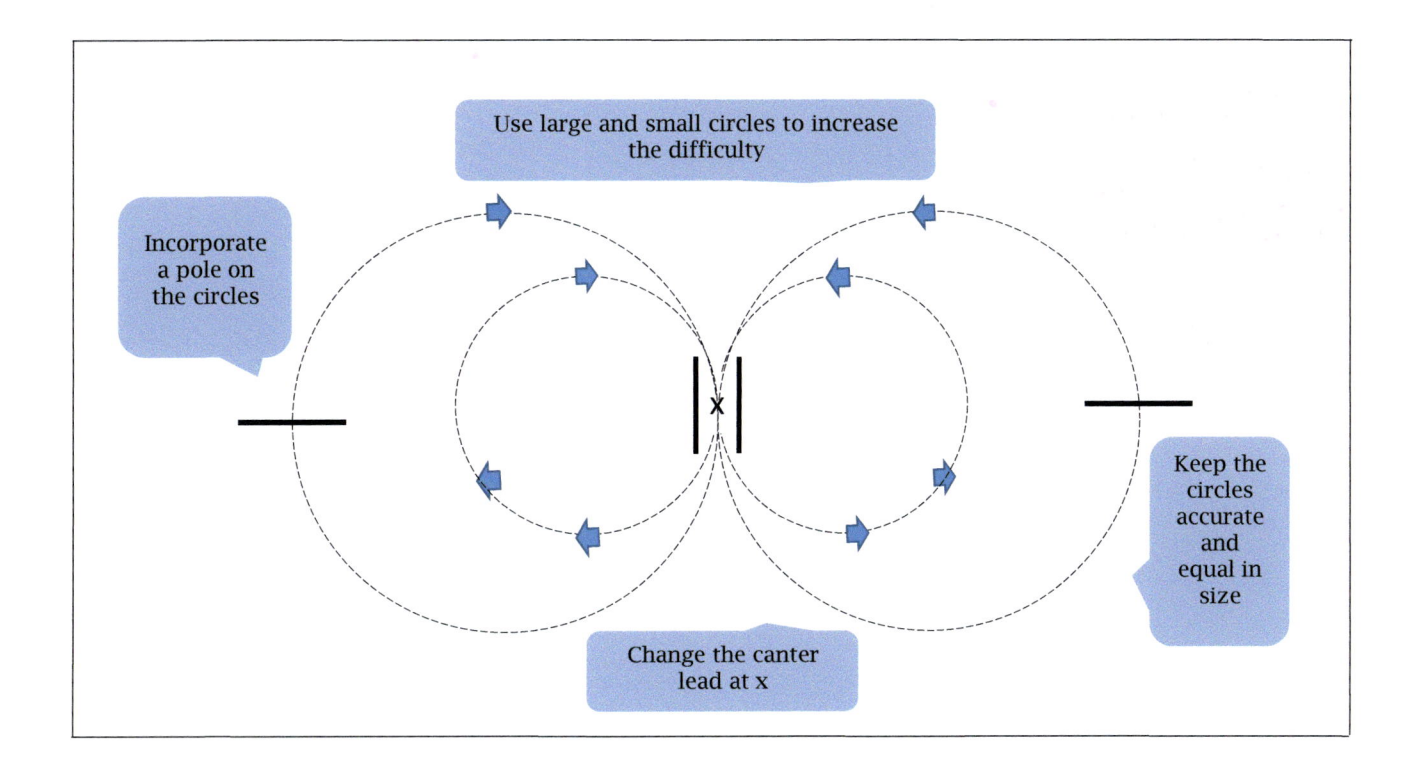

- Incorporate a pole on the circles
- Use large and small circles to increase the difficulty
- Keep the circles accurate and equal in size
- Change the canter lead at x

To increase the difficulty of exercise 6a, add two poles on the outside of the figure of 8.

In canter, alternate between riding the large figure of 8 including the poles, and riding the smaller figure of 8 with more collection.

Remember to ride the exercise on both reins.

Aims:
- ✓ To encourage the rider to look early for the pole to find the distance
- ✓ To maintain rhythm and balance over the pole
- ✓ To improve the accuracy of different size circles by planning ahead

Coach's tips:
- The rider must make sure their shoulders and hips follow the shape of the circles
- Keep the appropriate amount of bend for the size of the circles
- Return to trotting the exercise if the horse becomes tense

Progression:
Move on to exercise 6c for further suppleness.

Exercise 6c – Increasing suppleness and collection

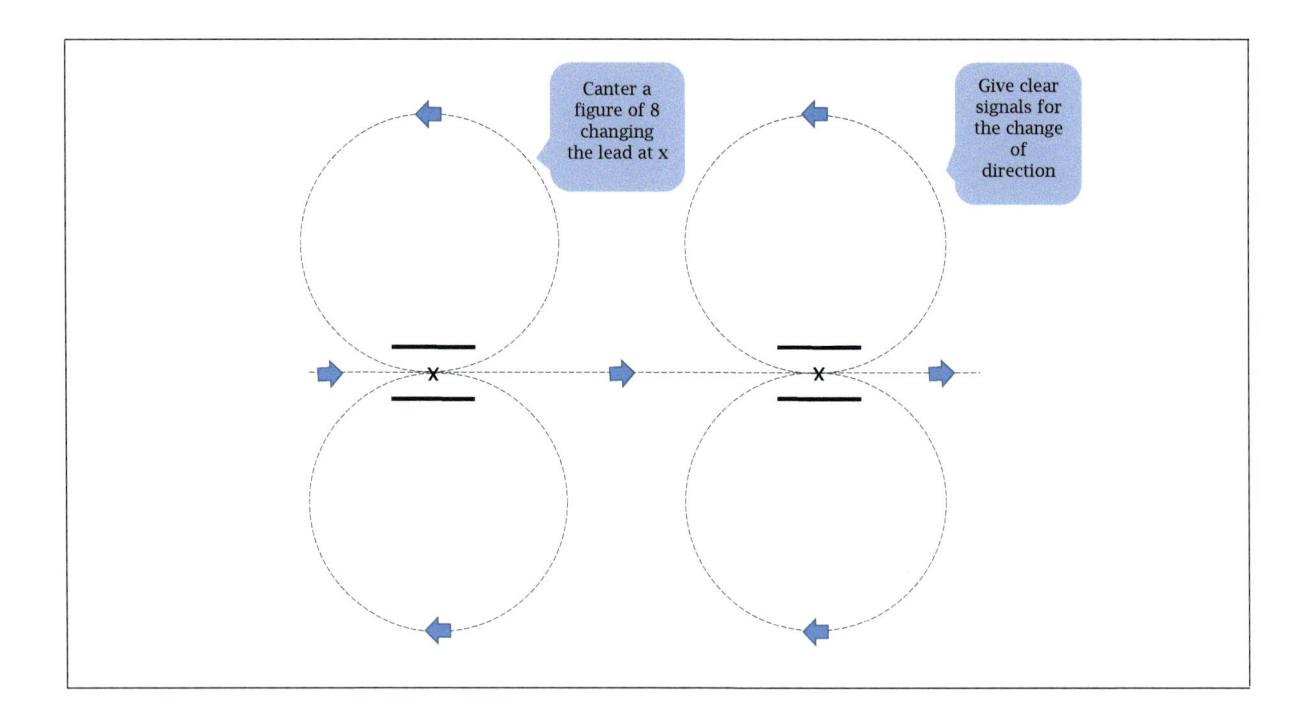

(Diagram: arena with two pairs of parallel poles on the centre line, each flanked by two dashed circles forming figures of 8, with X marked between each pair of poles.)

- Canter a figure of 8 changing the lead at x
- Give clear signals for the change of direction

To increase the difficulty of exercise 6, place two sets of parallel poles down the centre line.

It is best to try this exercise in trot before progressing to canter.

Ride straight down the centre line and ride a figure of 8 through the first pair of poles before going straight and repeating the figure of 8 at the second pair of poles.

If riding in canter, change the lead at x with a trot transition or flying change.

Aims:

- ✓ To encourage forward planning from the rider
- ✓ To make sure the figures of 8 are of equal size
- ✓ To increase the concentration of both rider and horse

Coach's tips:

- Remember to use the half-halts before changing the bend and changing the lead
- Follow the shape of the circles with your shoulders and hips

Exercise 7 – Serpentines and figures of 8

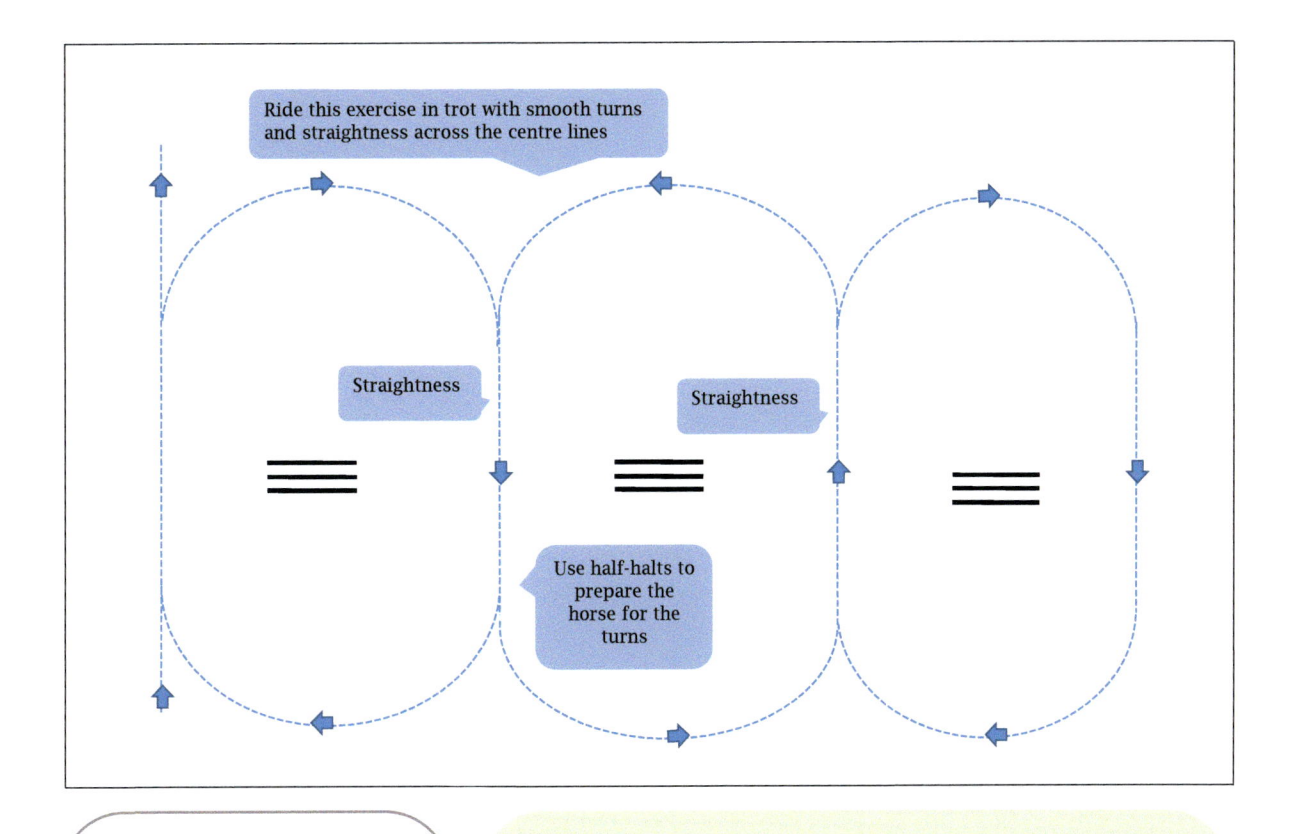

Ride this exercise in trot with smooth turns and straightness across the centre lines

Straightness

Straightness

Use half-halts to prepare the horse for the turns

Place three sets of trotting poles across the centre line.

Ride a three loop serpentine in trot changing the direction between the sets of poles.

Ride accurate turns giving plenty of time for a straight line across the centre.

Aims:
- ✓ To improve accuracy of riding turns and serpentines
- ✓ To develop straightness from the bend
- ✓ To encourage the rider to plan ahead and give clear directions

Coach's tips:
- Use half-halts to prepare your horse for the turns
- Look ahead to find your line
- If your horse rushes, then use trot/walk/trot transition to encourage relaxation

Progression:
Move on to exercise 7a when your horse feels supple and relaxed.

Exercise 7a - Serpentines and figures of 8

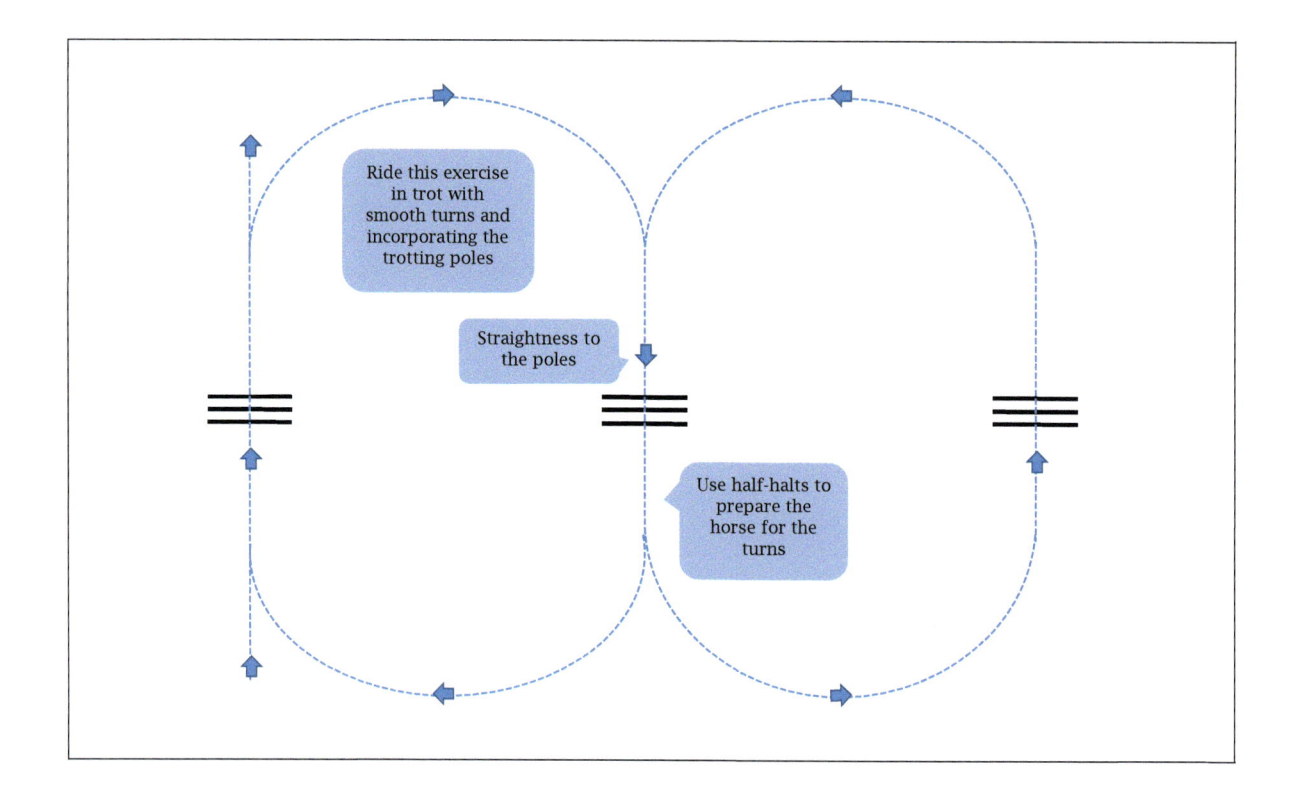

Diagram callouts:
- Ride this exercise in trot with smooth turns and incorporating the trotting poles
- Straightness to the poles
- Use half-halts to prepare the horse for the turns

Place three sets of trotting poles across the centre line.

Continue from exercise 7 by incorporating the three sets of trotting poles across the centre line forming a figure of 8.

Increase the difficulty by alternating between rising trot and posting trot (out of the saddle), focussing on maintaining the rhythm of trot.

Aims:
- ✓ To keep the same rhythm of trot throughout the exercise
- ✓ To improve suppleness and balance
- ✓ For the rider to maintain balance when changing between rising and posting trot

Coach's tips:
- Make sure you ride accurate lines to allow for straightness before, over and after the trotting poles
- Think and plan ahead at all times

Progression:
Move on to exercise 7b when you feel ready.

Exercise 7b - Serpentines and figures of 8

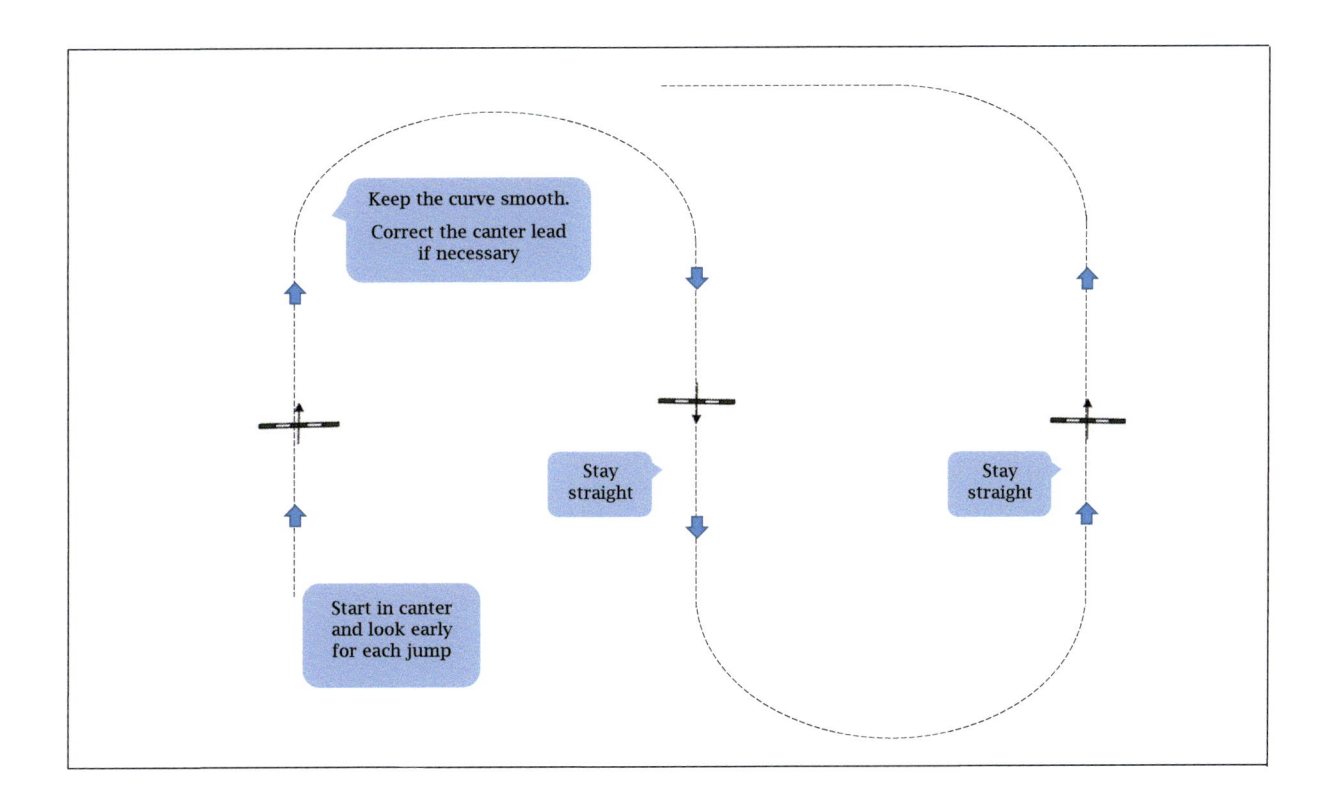

Diagram annotations:
- Keep the curve smooth. Correct the canter lead if necessary
- Stay straight
- Stay straight
- Start in canter and look early for each jump

Place three poles across the centre line.
Ride a two loop serpentine in canter incorporating the poles, focussing on smooth turns and straight lines over the poles.

Remember to change the bend and the canter lead on the turn, if necessary.

Change the poles into small jumps when you are ready.

Aims:
- ✓ To develop forward thinking from the rider
- ✓ To encourage the rider to feel the canter lead on landing and make any alterations quickly
- ✓ To improve rider/horse communication

Coach's tips:
- Use the half-halt to collect the horse on landing
- Make sure your hips and shoulders are parallel to the poles/jumps to encourage straightness

Progression:
To increase difficulty, move on to exercise 7c.

Exercise 7c - Serpentines and figures of 8

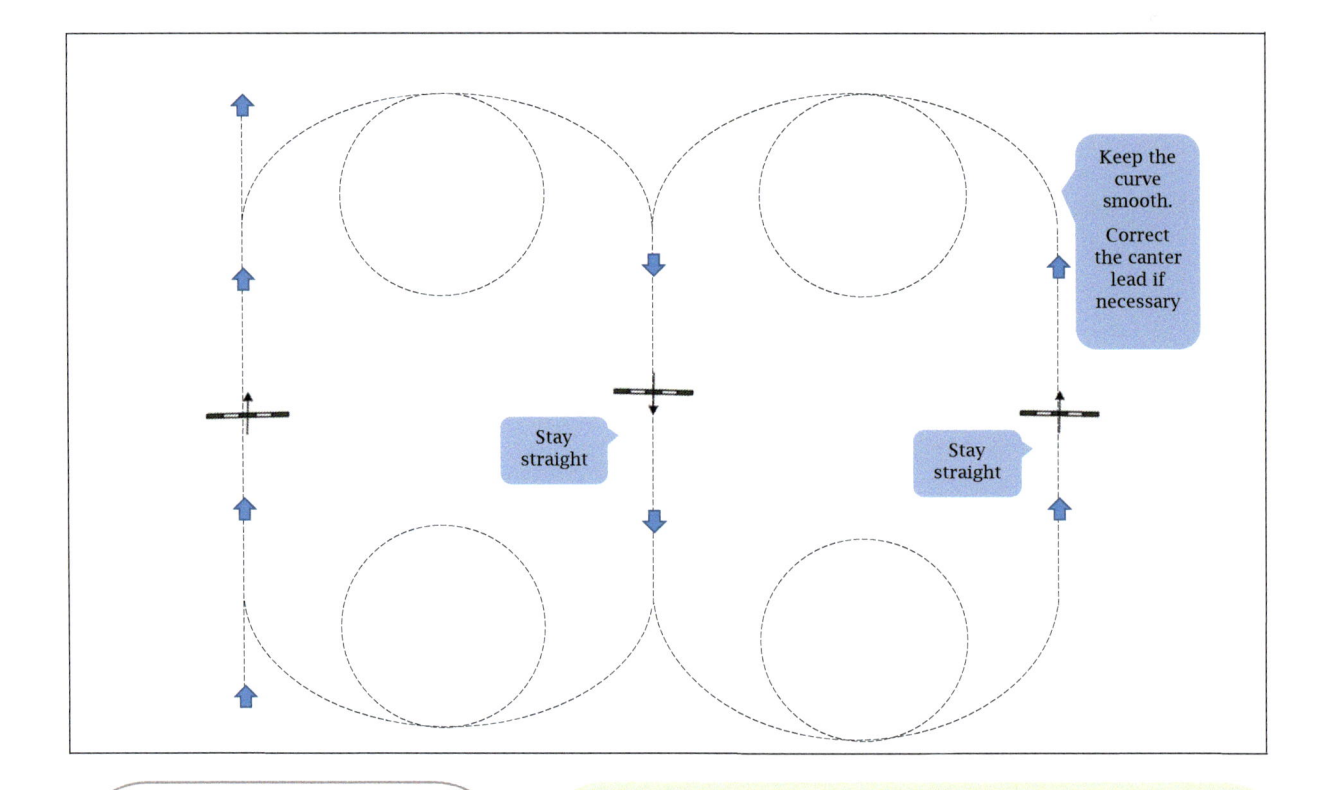

(Diagram shows arena with figure-of-8 pattern incorporating jumps, with annotations: "Keep the curve smooth. Correct the canter lead if necessary", "Stay straight", "Stay straight")

To increase the difficulty of exercise 7b, complete the figure of 8 with either poles or small jumps.

Remember to use the half halt to rebalance before each turn, and make sure to change the canter lead if necessary.

If your horse starts rushing use extra circles in either trot or canter to encourage relaxation.

Aims:
- ✓ To increase communication from rider to horse
- ✓ To improve suppleness and collection in canter
- ✓ To encourage the rider to think quickly and look early to find the distance to the jump

Coach's tips
- Be accurate on your turns to give yourself time for straightness to the jump
- Remember to ride straight after each jump as well as on the approach

Progression:
Move on to exercise 7d only when your horse feels totally confident.

Exercise 7d – Serpentine with bounces

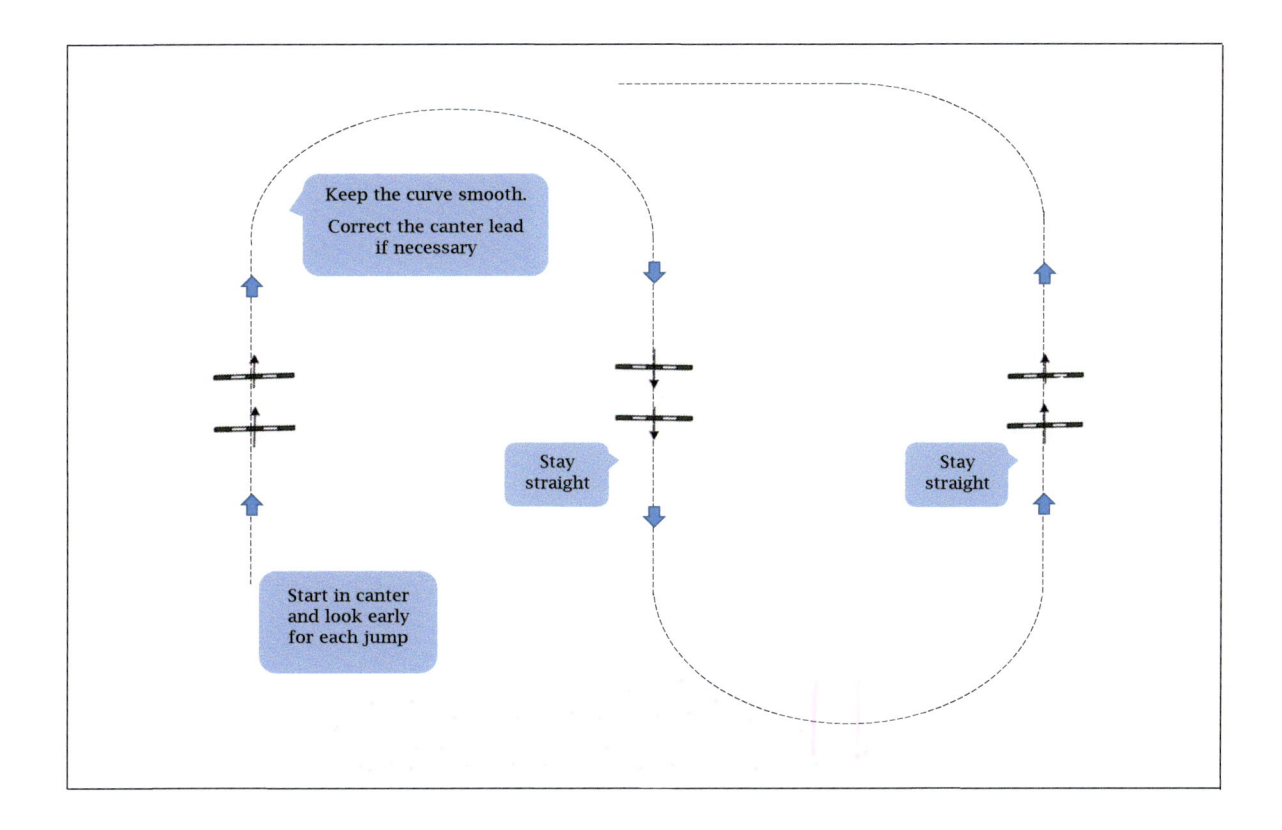

Diagram labels:
- Keep the curve smooth. Correct the canter lead if necessary
- Stay straight
- Stay straight
- Start in canter and look early for each jump

To increase the difficulty of exercise 7, change the three jumps to small bounces, if arena size allows for this.

Ride a two loop serpentine in canter remembering to approach straight, and ride away straight to create space and time.

You could use the same set up to make a figure of 8, changing direction over the middle bounce.

Aims:

- ✓ To further improve the rider's focus on straightness
- ✓ To strengthen the quality of the canter through using the bounce
- ✓ To encourage the rider to think quickly and plan ahead

Coach's tips:

- Remember to ride straight on approach and keep straight on landing
- The rider's hips and shoulders should always be parallel to the jump to help with the straightness
- If the horse becomes tense incorporate some circles to encourage relaxation

Exercise 8 - Transitions and riding diagonals

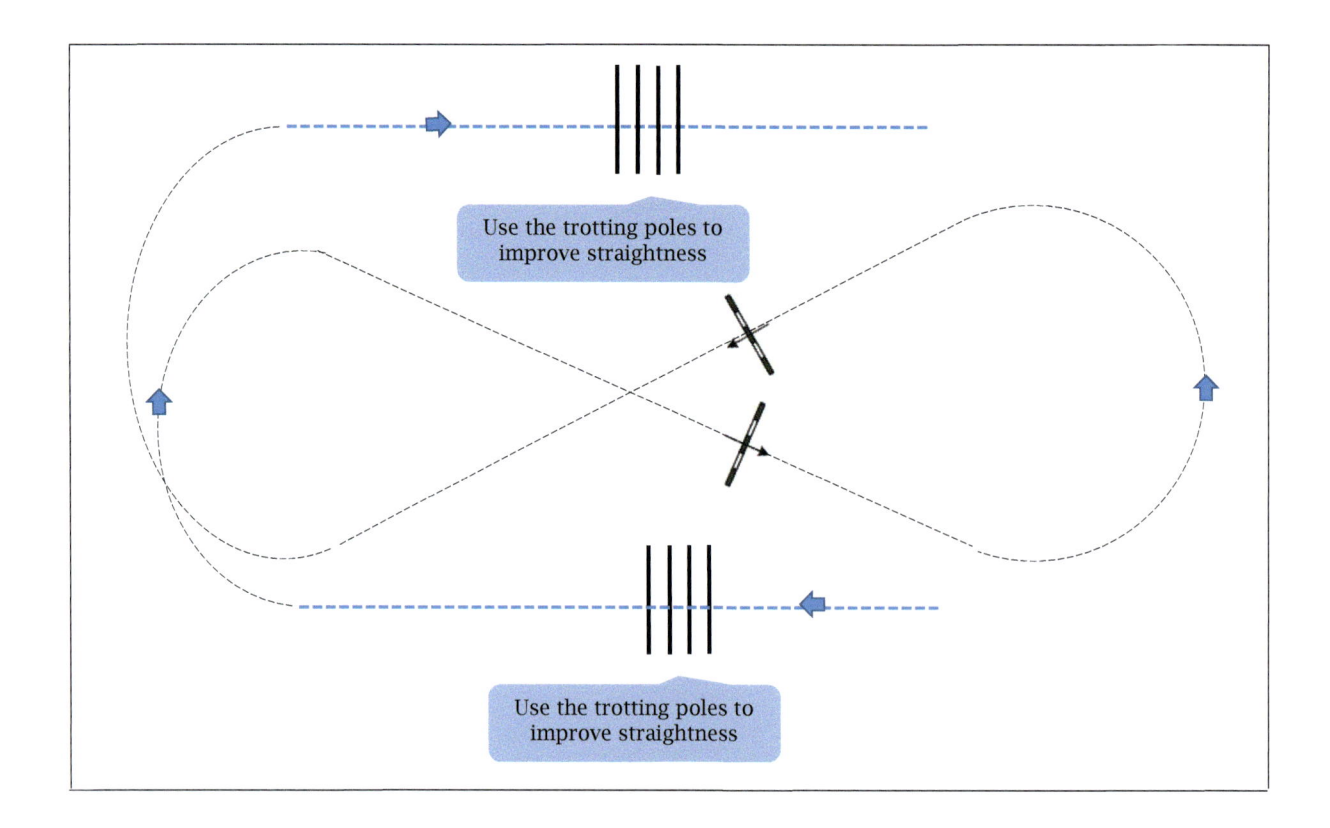

Use the trotting poles to improve straightness

Use the trotting poles to improve straightness

Place two sets of trotting poles on the long sides of the arena. Then place two small jumps across the diagonal.

Start on the right rein over the trotting poles. Make a transition into canter at the beginning of the turn, then canter across both diagonals to the jumps. Make a smooth transition to trot on the turn to be straight and in balance again for the trotting poles to finish.
Repeat from the opposite direction.

Aims:

- ✓ To ride straight lines both over the trotting poles and across the diagonal
- ✓ To encourage the rider to look early to find the line
- ✓ To ensure the horse is relaxed by using the trotting poles to finish

Coach's Tips:

- Be ready to prevent the horse from falling in or out on the turns
- Leaving the turn too early will cause the horse to be unbalanced and crooked across the diagonal to the jump

Exercise 9 – Straightness across the diagonal

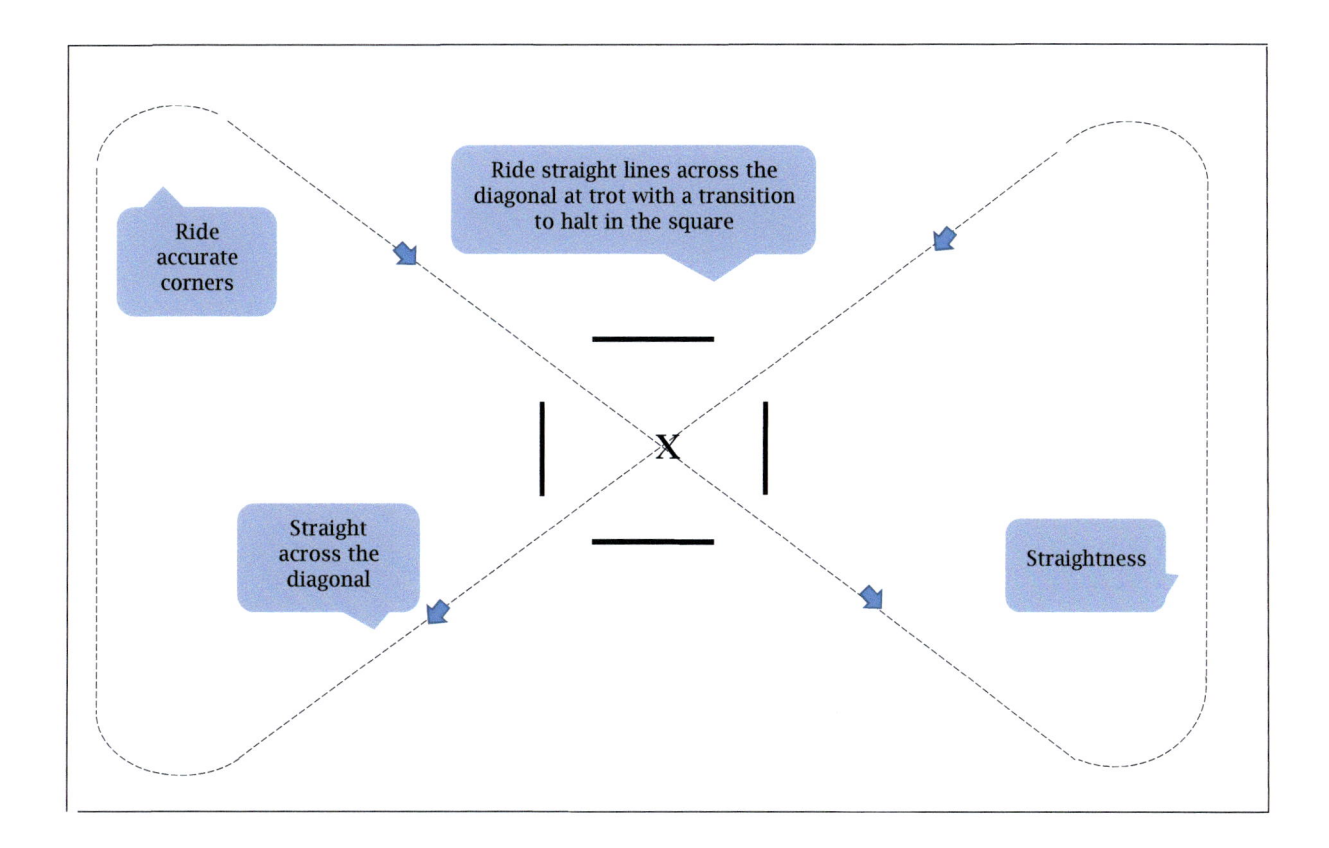

Diagram labels:
- Ride accurate corners
- Ride straight lines across the diagonal at trot with a transition to halt in the square
- Straight across the diagonal
- Straightness
- X (centre with four poles forming a square with open corners)

Place four poles in the centre of the arena in a square with open corners.

Ride this exercise in canter, changing the lead in the box at x with a trot transition.

You can also choose to do a transition to walk, or even halt at x, if you want to vary the exercise.

The focus is for the rider to be straight across the diagonal.

Aims:
- ✓ To improve preparation on the corners for straightness across the diagonal
- ✓ To use transitions to increase attention from the horse
- ✓ To encourage the rider to plan ahead

Coach's tips:
- Use the half-halt before the corners to collect the canter
- Look early to find the line to enter and exit the box straight

Progression:
To increase difficulty, try and make your change of lead happen quicker, but without forcing it. Use a flying change when your horse feels ready.

Exercise 9a - Straightness on the centre line

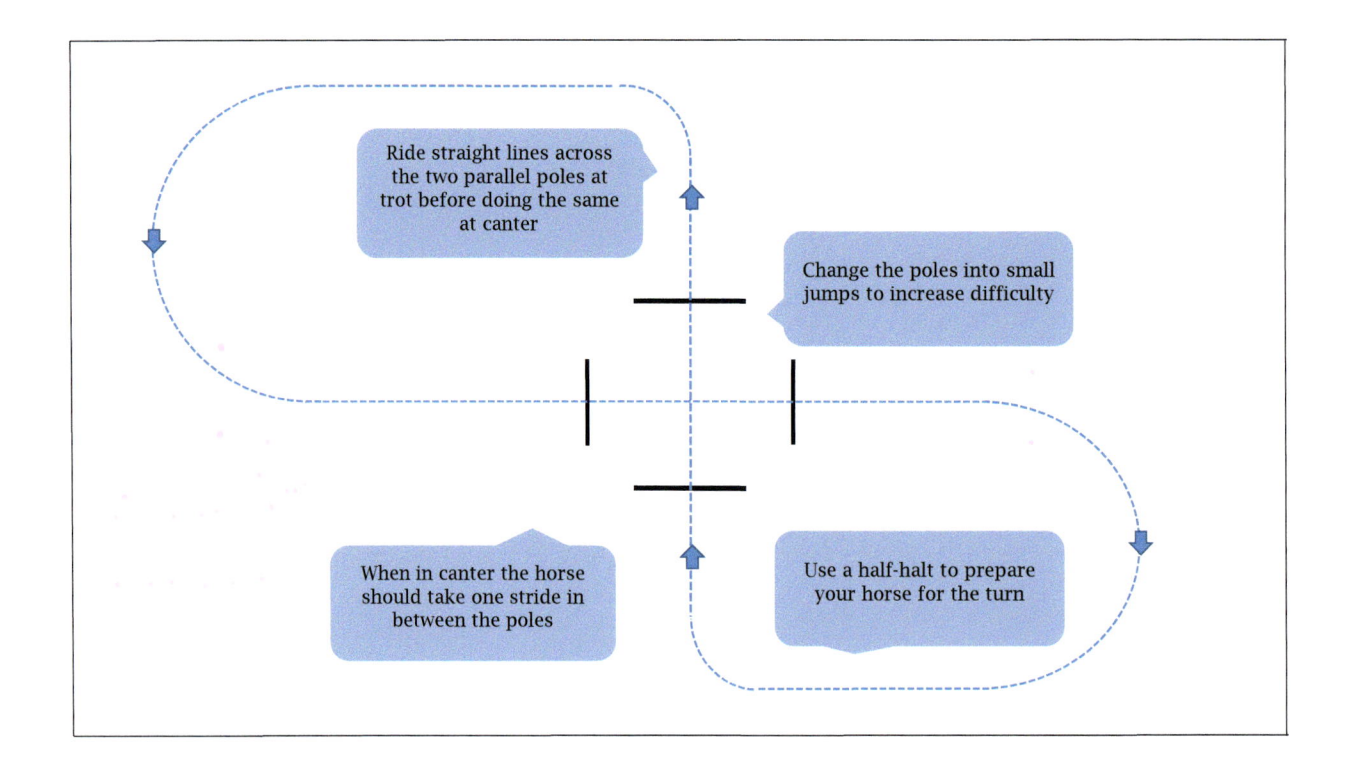

Diagram annotations:
- Ride straight lines across the two parallel poles at trot before doing the same at canter
- Change the poles into small jumps to increase difficulty
- When in canter the horse should take one stride in between the poles
- Use a half-halt to prepare your horse for the turn

Place four poles in the centre of the arena in a square, one canter stride apart. Make sure the distance suits your horse's length of canter stride.

Start by riding this exercise in trot, making smooth turns and keeping straight before, over and after the poles.

When the horse feels relaxed, repeat the exercise in canter changing the lead after the poles.

Aims:
- ✓ To improve straightness across, and down, the centre line
- ✓ To encourage the rider to plan ahead
- ✓ To improve accuracy of turns

Coach's tips:
- Alternate between riding the exercise at trot and canter to keep the horse relaxed
- The rider should have both their hips and shoulders parallel to the poles to help with straightness

Progression:
Change the poles into small jumps to increase the difficulty, remember to alter the distance to suit the canter stride.

Exercise 9b – Riding accurate circles

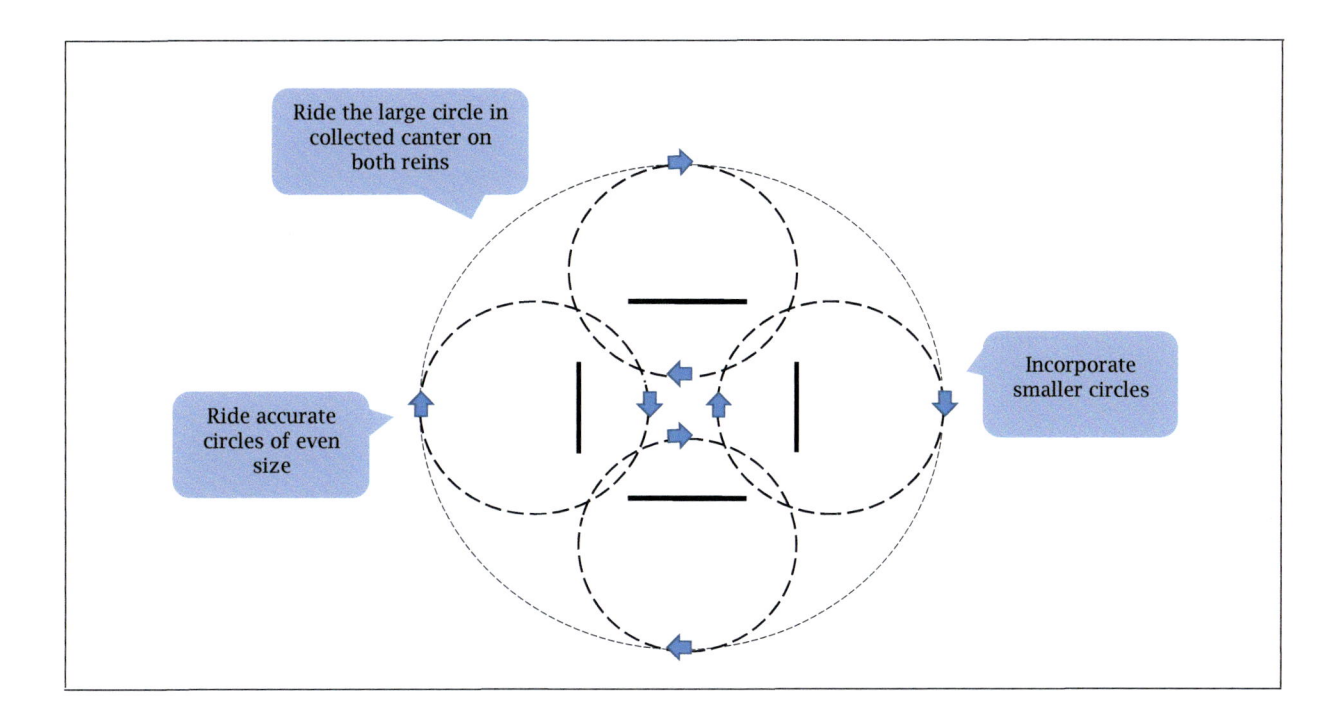

Ride the large circle in collected canter on both reins

Incorporate smaller circles

Ride accurate circles of even size

Place four poles in the centre of the arena in a square with open corners.

Start by cantering a large circle around all four poles. When the canter feels relaxed with a soft inside bend incorporate small circles around each pole.

Keep alternating between the large circle and the smaller circles.

Ride this exercise on both reins.

Aims:
- ✓ To increase the collection of the canter on the smaller circles
- ✓ To improve suppleness and balance
- ✓ To be aware of the appropriate amount of bend needed for the size of the circle

Coach's tips:
- Make occasional transitions to trot to keep the horse relaxed
- Follow the shape of the circles with your body and support with your inside leg on the girth on the smaller circles

Progression;
Move on to exercise 9c when you feel ready.

Exercise 9c - Riding accurate circles

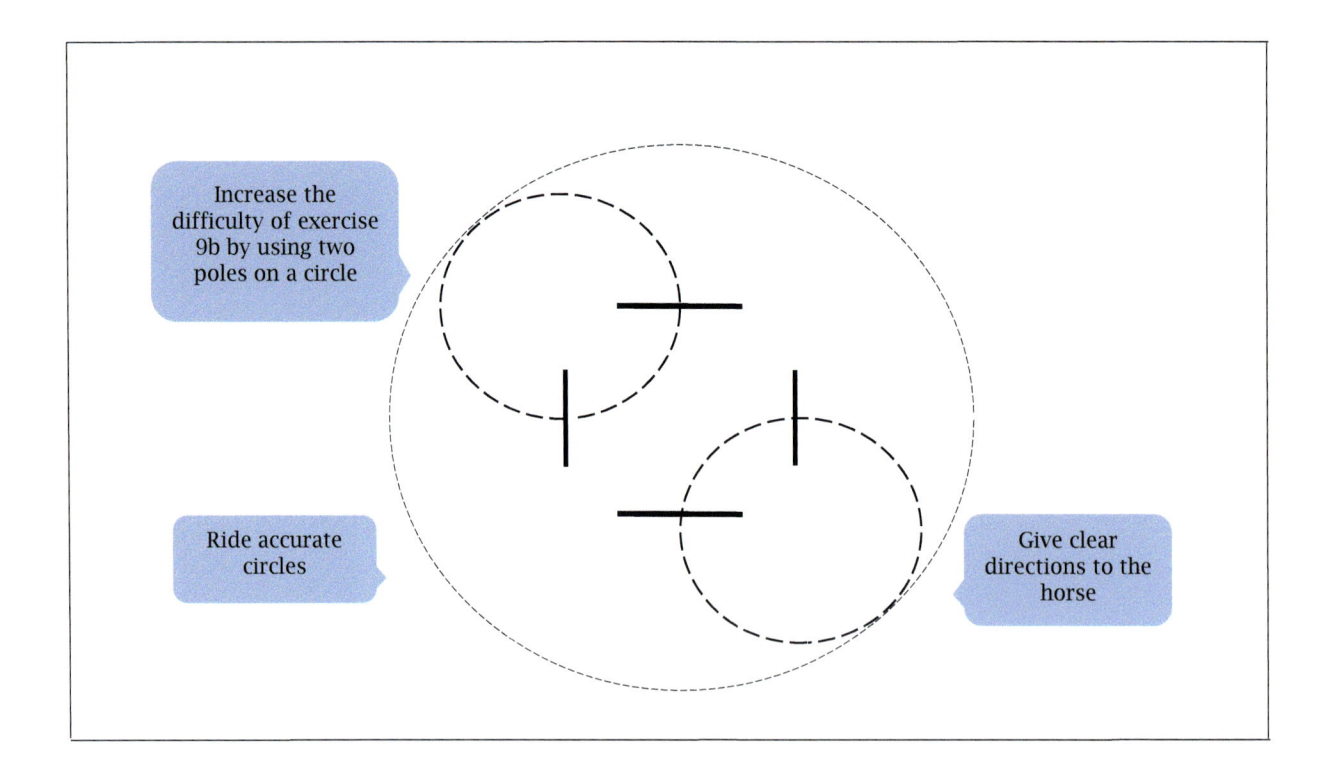

Diagram callouts:
- Increase the difficulty of exercise 9b by using two poles on a circle
- Ride accurate circles
- Give clear directions to the horse

To increase the difficulty of exercise 9b, incorporate the poles on the small circles.

Start by cantering the large circle around all four poles. When you are ready, canter a small circle incorporating two of the poles. Move on to the large circle before riding another small circle over two more poles.

Make sure you find the line on the circle that suits your horse's length of canter stride.

Repeat on both reins.

Aims:
- ✓ To improve accuracy from the rider in riding circles
- ✓ To discover where the small circle works for your horse's length of stride
- ✓ To increase rider/horse communication

Coach's tips:

- If your horse is finding it difficult then return to trot until the horse understands the route before trying again in canter
- Don't feel rushed, give your horse time to learn

Exercise 10 - Straightness and square turns

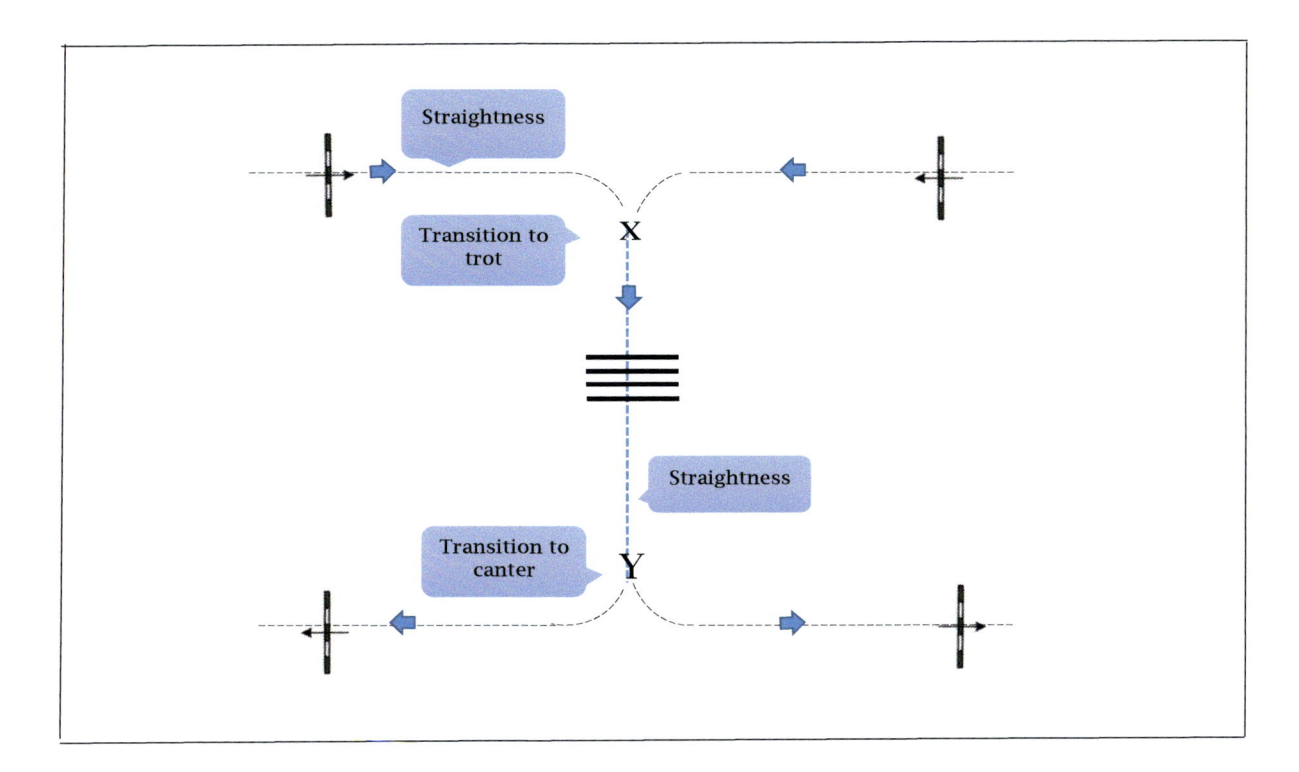

Place four small jumps in a large square with at least 6 canter strides between them. Also place four trotting poles across the centre line.

Start in canter on the right rein over the small jump, landing straight. Make a square turn and a transition to trot at X.
Focus on the straightness to the trotting poles and make a transition to canter at Y. Then make a square turn to the left in order to be straight for the next jump.

Repeat from both directions.

Aims:

- ✓ To improve accuracy of transitions
- ✓ To increase rider/horse communication
- ✓ To encourage the rider to prepare early for the turns
- ✓ To keep the horse's attention

Coach's tips:

- Stay relaxed and don't force the transitions
- Use a quiet voice to back up your instructions

Progression:
Move on to exercise 10a when you feel ready.

Exercise 10a – Straightness and square turns

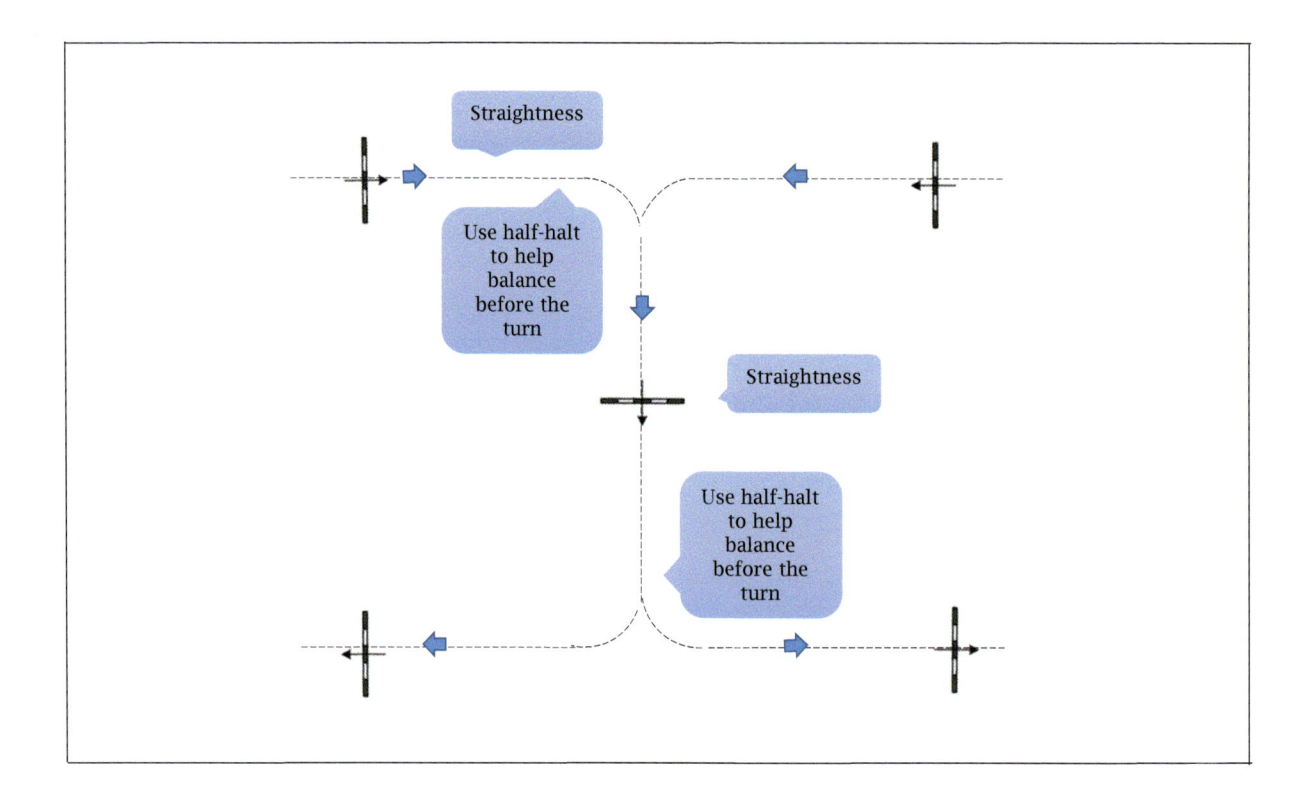

Diagram labels:
- Straightness
- Use half-halt to help balance before the turn
- Straightness
- Use half-halt to help balance before the turn

Place four small jumps in a large square with at least 6 strides between them. Then place another small jump across the centre line.

Start in canter on the right rein over the small jump, land straight and make a square turn. Focus on the straightness to the jump on the centre line and stay straight on landing. Make another square turn to the left in order to be straight for the next jump.

You can now ride this exercise as a figure of 8, remembering the square turns.

Aims:
- ✓ To encourage the rider to plan ahead
- ✓ To increase rider/horse communication
- ✓ To stop the horse from anticipating the jump and the direction
- ✓ To improve balance on the turns

Coach's tips:
- Remember to use a half-halt to rebalance the canter before the turns
- Look early to find the line and the distance to the jump
- Keep your shoulders and hips parallel to the jump to ensure straightness on approach and away from the jump

Exercise 11 - Straightness, transitions and square turns

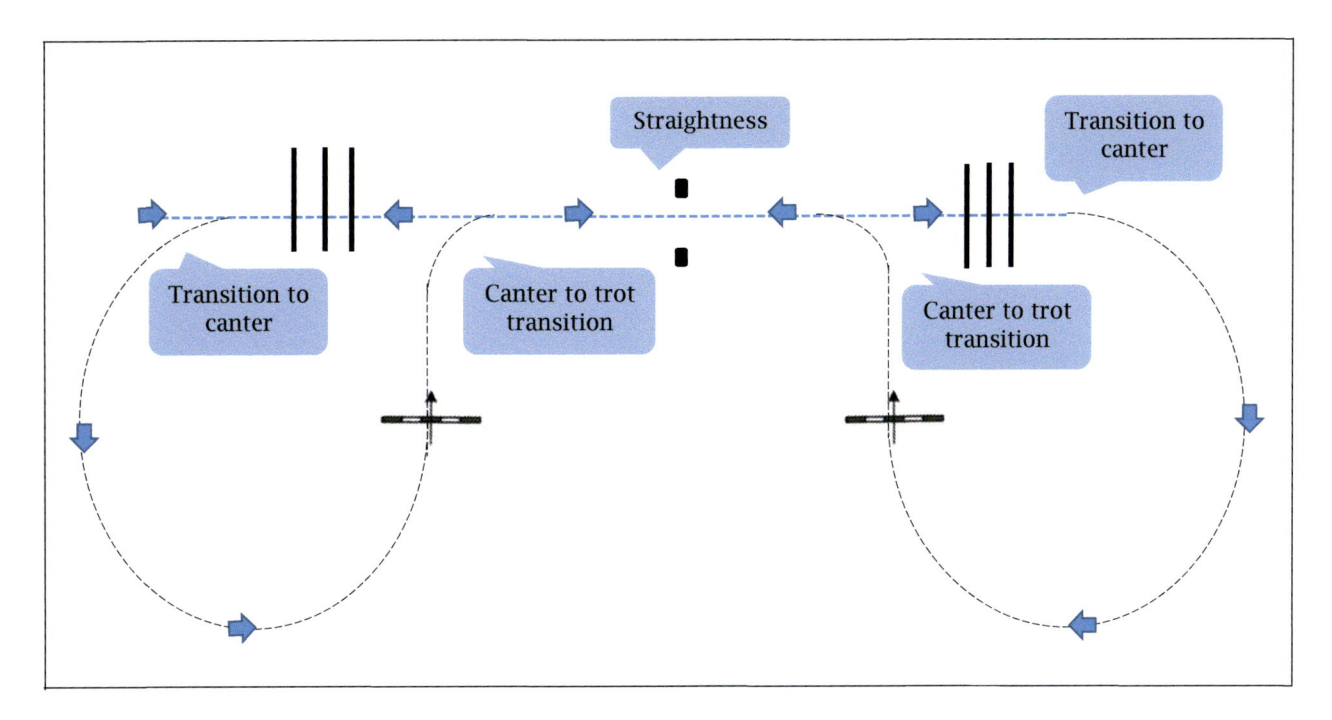

Diagram labels:
- Straightness
- Transition to canter
- Transition to canter
- Canter to trot transition
- Canter to trot transition

Place two sets of trotting poles down the long side of the arena with cones or blocks to help with the straightness. Also place two small jumps at a right angle on the centre line.

Start in trot over both sets of trotting poles, focussing on the straightness. Then make a transition into canter and ride a turn back to the small jump. Make a transition to trot on approach to the straight line, proceed to the trotting poles before making a transition into canter and turning back to the next jump.

Aims:

- ✓ To improve straightness and square turns
- ✓ To encourage the rider to plan ahead
- ✓ To increase rider/horse communication
- ✓ To improve transitions and encourage the horse to listen

Coach's tips:

- Stay relaxed and don't force the transitions, use a quiet voice to back up your instructions
- Be aware of the horse falling in or out on the turns and be ready to correct the bend if necessary

Progression:
Move on to exercise 11a when you feel ready.

Exercise 11a - Straightness and square turns

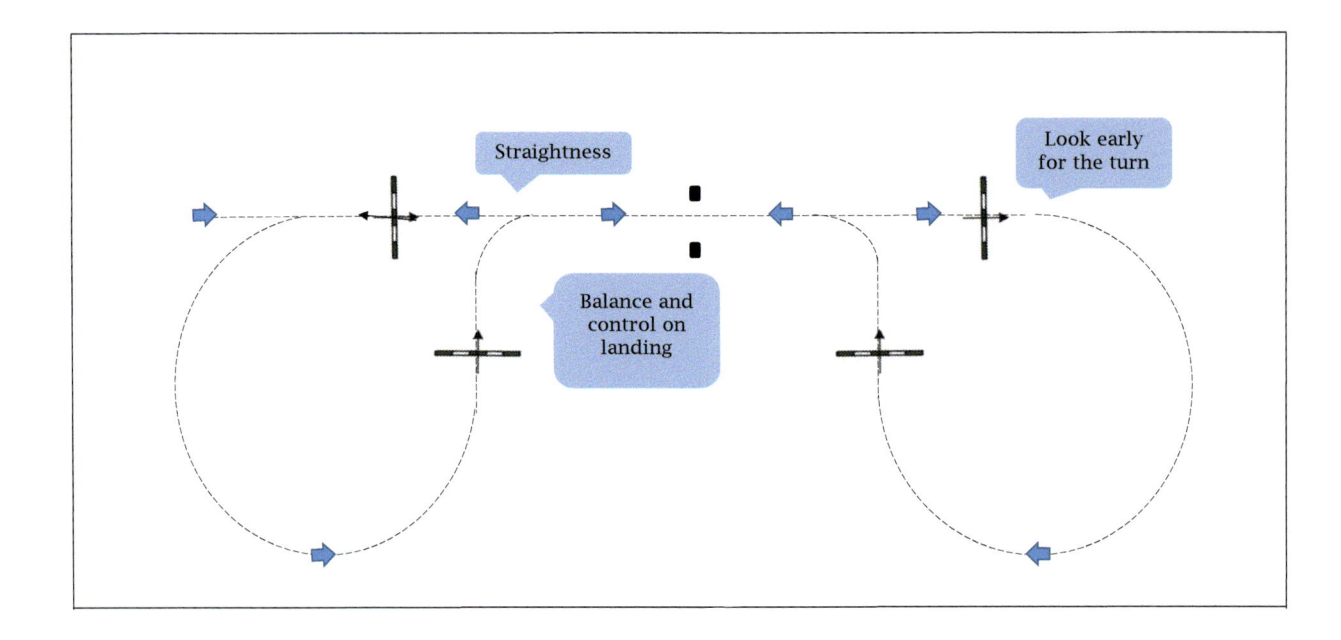

Diagram labels: Straightness · Look early for the turn · Balance and control on landing

Place two small jumps on the long side of the arena with cones or blocks to help with the straightness. Also put two small jumps at a right angle on the centre line.

Increase the difficulty of exercise 11 by starting in canter on the right rein, focussing on the straight line down the long side over the two jumps. Remember to correct the canter lead early (if required) before turning back to the next jump, and then ride back on to the straight line to the jump again.
Finish by turning back left to the next jump and being straight again through the cones/blocks.

Aims:

- ✓ To encourage the rider to plan ahead
- ✓ To increase rider/horse communication
- ✓ To stop the horse from anticipating the jump and the direction
- ✓ To improve balance on the turns

Coach's tips:

- Remember to use a half-halt to rebalance the canter before the turns
- Look early to find the line and the distance to the jump
- Keep your shoulders and hips parallel to the jump to ensure straightness on approach and away from the jump

Exercise 12 – Accurate circles and suppleness

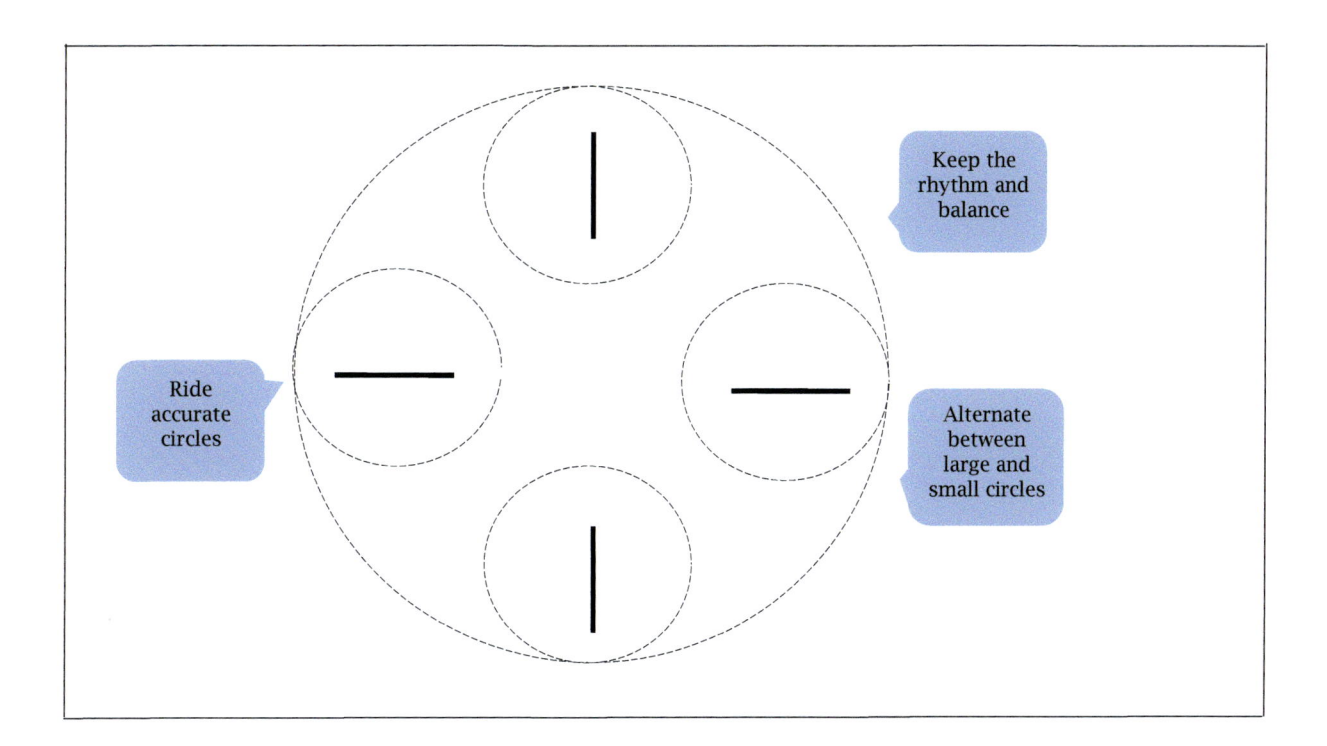

Callouts on diagram:
- Ride accurate circles
- Keep the rhythm and balance
- Alternate between large and small circles

Place four poles in a star shape in the centre of the arena with a gap of approx. 24ft (8 paces) between the inside ends of the poles.

Start on either rein by cantering a large circle around all four poles. When the canter feels balanced start incorporating a small circle around each pole.

Alternate between the large circle and the smaller circles. The small circles should all be of equal size.

Ride this exercise on both reins.

Aims:
- ✓ To keep the horse in a consistent rhythm, both on the small and large circles
- ✓ To ride accurate circles
- ✓ To improve collection on the smaller circles

Coach's tips:
- Be aware of the horse falling in or out on the circles
- Make sure you have the appropriate amount of bend for the size of the circle

Progression:
To increase difficulty put some variation into the length of the canter stride but keep the rhythm the same.

Exercise 12a - Riding accurate circles to poles/jumps

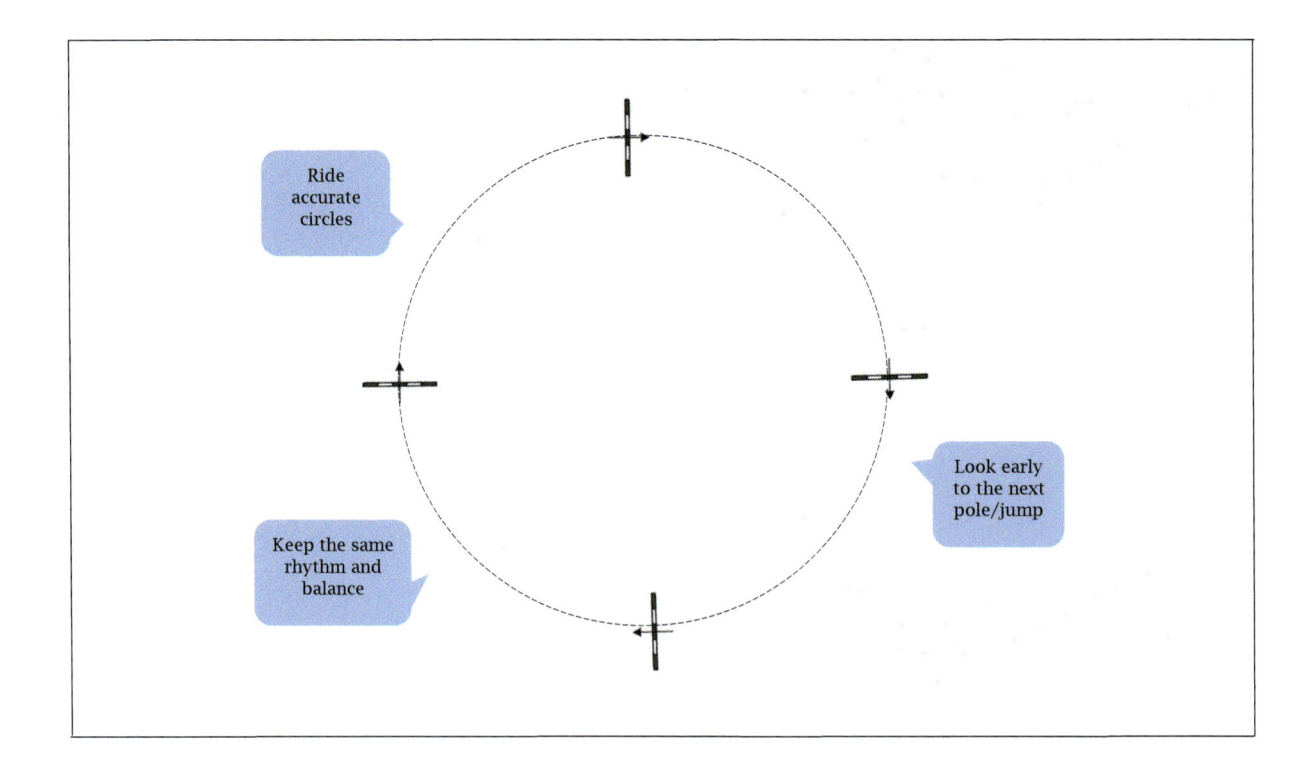

Diagram callouts:
- Ride accurate circles
- Look early to the next pole/jump
- Keep the same rhythm and balance

Place four poles in a star shape in the centre of the arena with a gap of approx. 30ft (10 paces) between the inside ends of the poles.

Start by riding the circle over the poles at trot. When the horse is relaxed proceed at canter.

Make sure the horse is central to each pole and has the same number of strides between each pole.

Repeat on both reins

Aims:
- ✓ To encourage the rider to plan ahead
- ✓ To keep the horse in a consistent length of stride
- ✓ To ride accurate circles

Coach's tips
- Be aware of the horse falling in or out on the circle
- Look early to the next pole/jump to find the distance and make small adjustments if necessary

Progression:
To increase the difficulty, change the poles into small jumps.

Exercise 12b - Riding accurate circles to poles/jumps

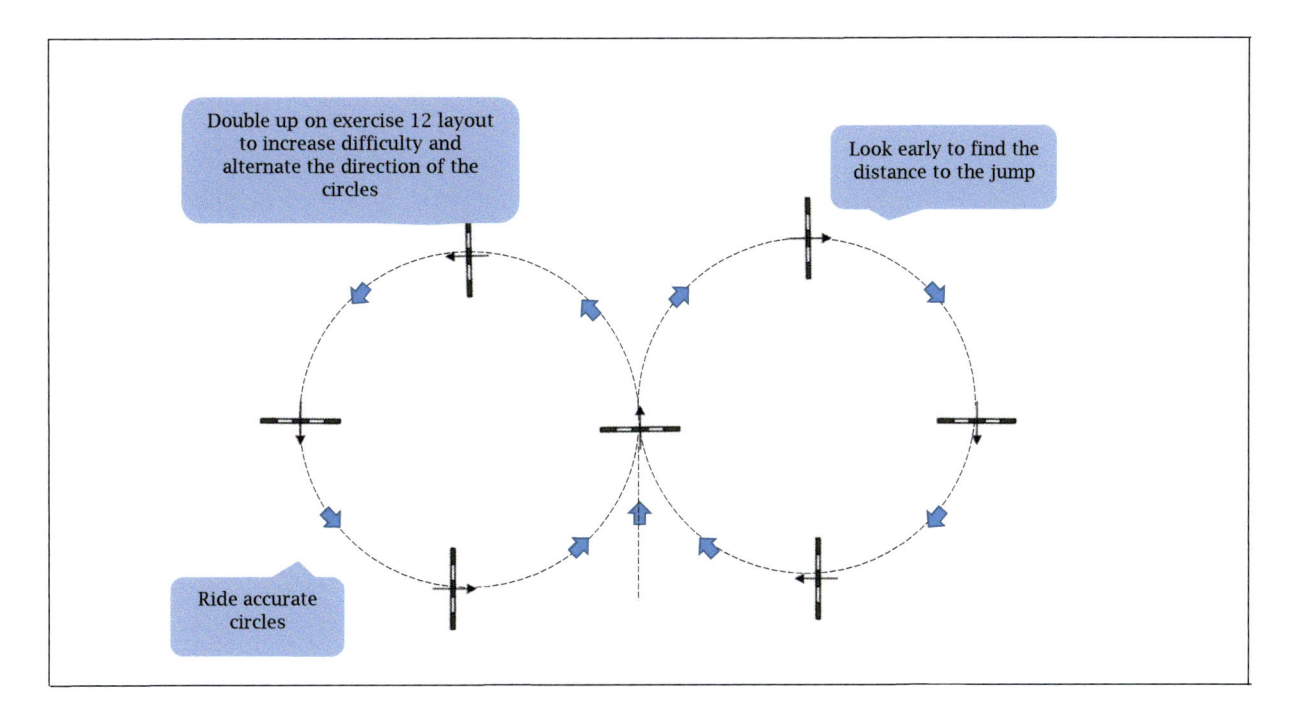

Double up on exercise 12 layout to increase difficulty and alternate the direction of the circles

Look early to find the distance to the jump

Ride accurate circles

Place seven poles in a figure of 8 shape in the centre of the arena with a gap of approx. 30ft (10 paces) between the inside ends of the poles.

Start the exercise in trot to find your route before proceeding in canter.
Ride the circle of poles the same as exercise 12c, changing the rein over the centre pole, remembering to change the canter lead.

If your horse finds it difficult, make it less demanding by riding larger circles nearer the outer edge of the poles.

Aims:
- To keep the horse in a consistent length of stride on the circles
- To ride accurate circles in balance
- To prepare the horse for the change of direction
- To encourage the rider to look early

Coach's tips:
- Be aware of the horse anticipating the direction in the centre
- If your horse gets tense, then repeat the exercise at trot to encourage relaxation
- Stay relaxed and give your horse time to learn

Progression:
To increase difficulty, change the poles into small jumps.

Exercise 12c - Castle exercise for suppleness

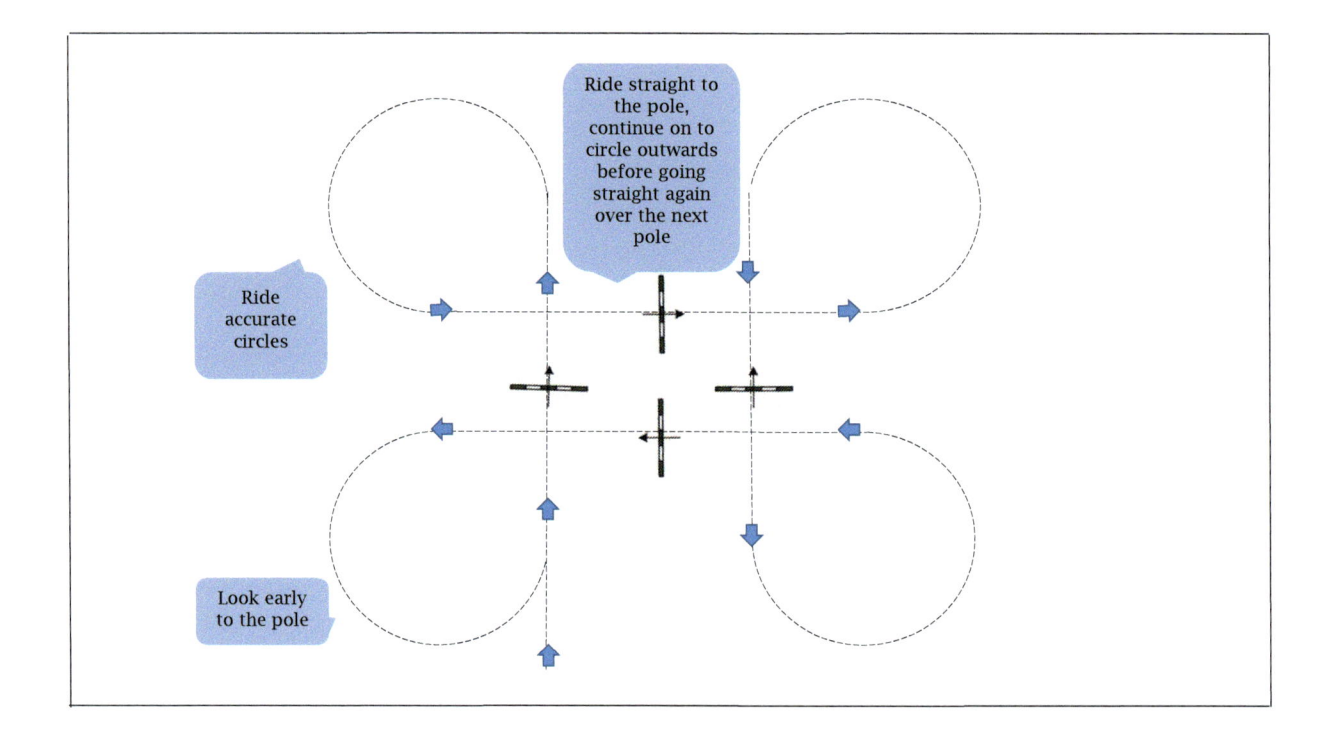

Diagram labels:
- Ride straight to the pole, continue on to circle outwards before going straight again over the next pole
- Ride accurate circles
- Look early to the pole

Place four poles in a star shape in the centre of the arena with a gap of approx. 12ft (4 paces) between the inside ends of the poles.

Ride straight over a pole and continue on a circle turning outward, exit the circle on a straight line to proceed over the next pole.
Continue with another outward circle before exiting straight over the next pole.
Continue in the same way until you have completed the exercise.

This exercise works best when started in trot to establish the route before repeating in canter.

Aims:

- ✓ To develop forward planning from the rider
- ✓ To increase suppleness and balance
- ✓ To encourage the horse to listen instead of rushing to the pole

Coach's tips:

- The rider needs to look early towards the next pole allowing the hips and shoulders to turn when you turn your head
- Return to trot if the horse finds it too difficult in canter
- Give the horse time to learn

Progression:
When you feel comfortable, you can make the poles into four small jumps.

Exercise 12d – Suppleness and concentration

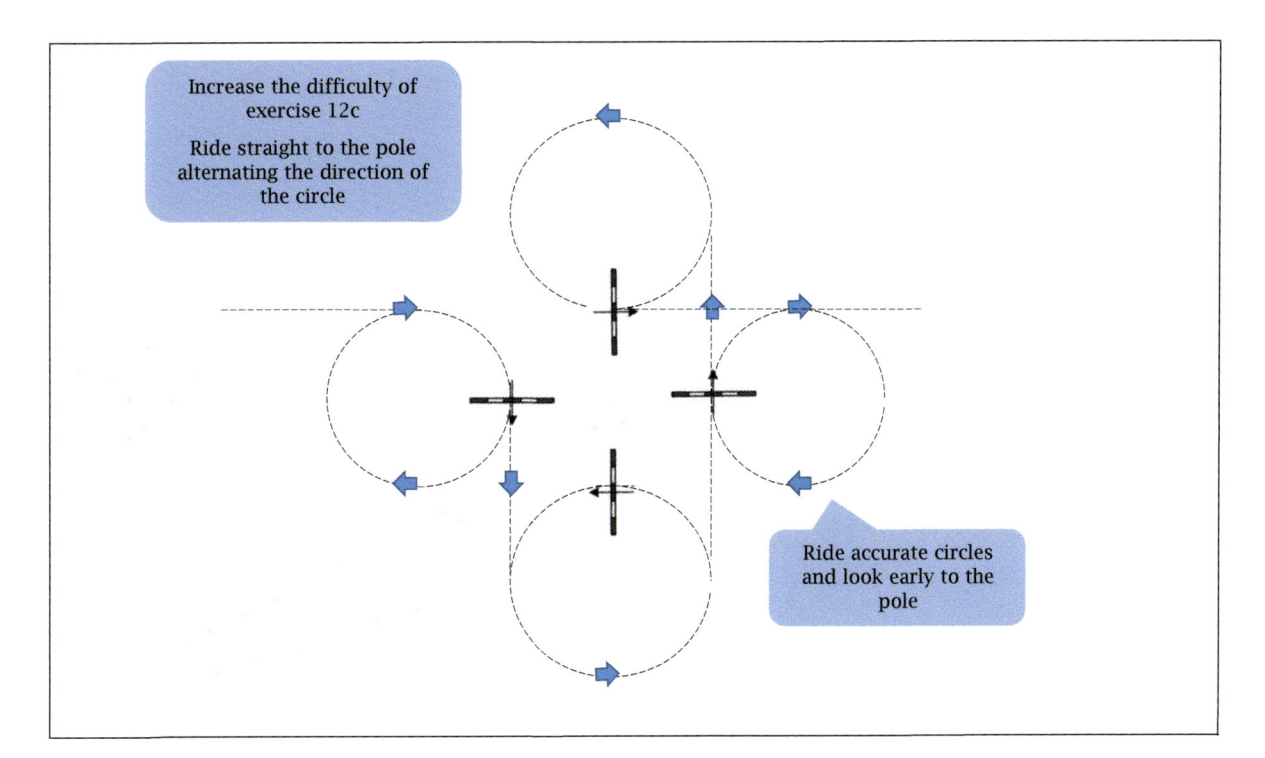

Diagram labels:
- Increase the difficulty of exercise 12c. Ride straight to the pole alternating the direction of the circle
- Ride accurate circles and look early to the pole

To increase the difficulty of exercise 12c, alternate the direction of the circles.

Canter a circle to the right over the first pole circling outwards, then exit straight and canter a circle to the left over the next pole circling inwards. Keep following the same process until you have finished the exercise.

Repeat the exercise in reverse.

Aims:

- ✓ To have clear communication with the horse and plan ahead
- ✓ To ride accurate circles
- ✓ To improve collection

Coach's tips:

- Be aware of the horse anticipating the direction
- Support horse to stop him falling in or out on the circle
- Follow the shape of the circles with your hips and shoulders

Progression:
To increase difficulty, change the poles into small jumps.

Exercise 13 - 90 degree turns and straightness

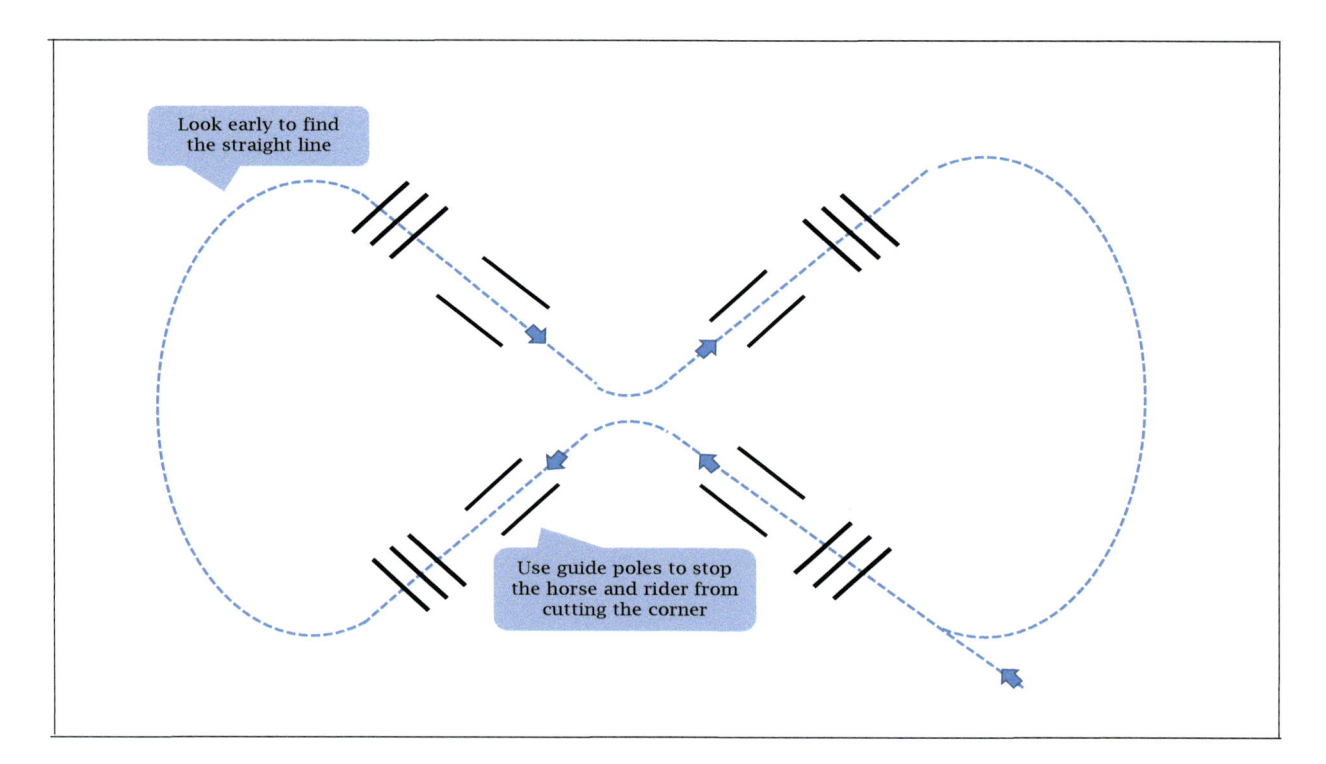

Look early to find the straight line

Use guide poles to stop the horse and rider from cutting the corner

Place four sets of trotting poles in the shape of an X. Then add guide poles to help you keep the shape of the exercise.

Start this exercise in trot over one of the sets of trotting poles, make a square turn. Ensure consistent straightness is achieved using the guide poles before and after the trotting poles.
Make a smooth turn on the short side of the arena.

Repeat in the opposite direction.

Aims:

- ✓ To stay in rhythm and balance
- ✓ To be accurate on the square turns giving more time for straightness to the poles
- ✓ To keep the rider thinking and planning ahead

Coach's tips:

- Collect the horse before each turn to maintain balance
- Make sure you are straight before, over and after the poles
- Look early to find the straight line

Progression:
Move on to exercise 13a when your horse feels ready.

Exercise 13a - 90 degree turns and straightness

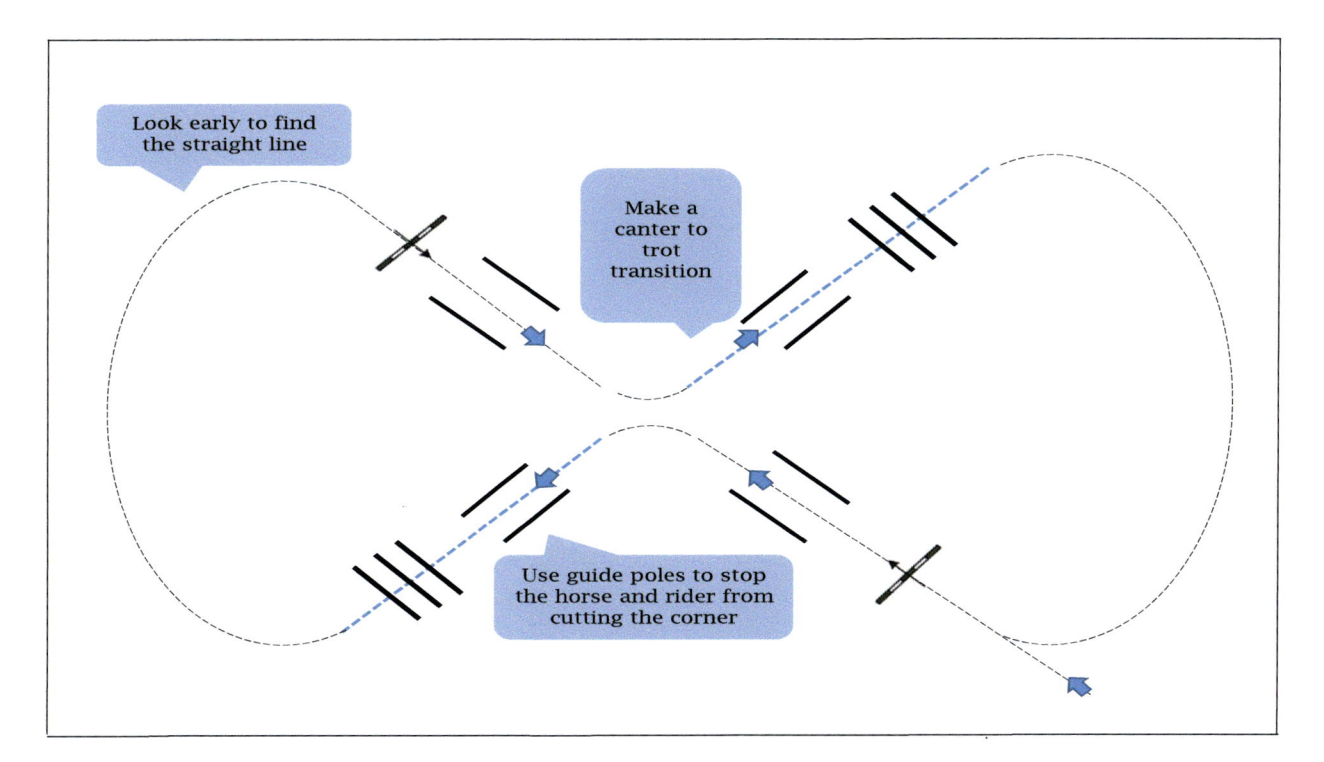

Diagram labels:
- Look early to find the straight line
- Make a canter to trot transition
- Use guide poles to stop the horse and rider from cutting the corner

To increase the difficulty of exercise 13, change two of the sets of trotting poles into small jumps keeping the shape of an X.

Start this exercise in canter to a small jump staying straight through the guide poles. Make a transition to trot before making a square turn and going straight to the trotting poles.
Make a transition into canter on the short side of the arena and make a smooth turn to the next jump. Land straight and make another trot transition to the trotting poles to finish.
Repeat in the opposite direction.

Aims:

- ✓ To encourage the rider to plan ahead
- ✓ To execute smooth transitions
- ✓ To be accurate on the turns and focus on straightness
- ✓ To stop the horse from anticipating the direction

Coach's tips:

- Support the horse with your inside leg to stop the horse from cutting the corner
- Use a quiet voice to back up aids if necessary
- Don't let it feel rushed

Progression:
When the horse feels relaxed move on to exercise 13b.

Exercise 13b - 90 degree turns and straightness

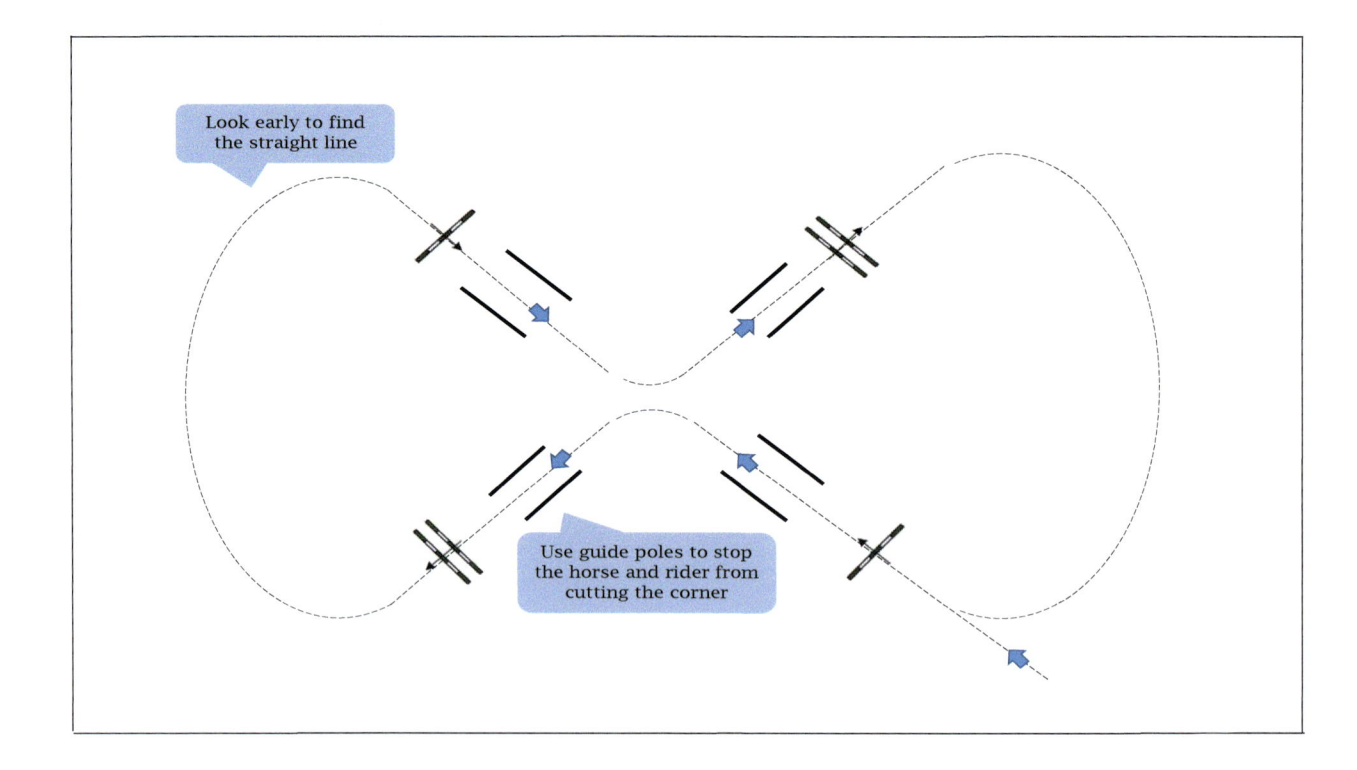

Look early to find the straight line

Use guide poles to stop the horse and rider from cutting the corner

To increase the difficulty of exercise 13a, change the remaining two sets of trotting poles into small jumps keeping the shape of an X.

Start this exercise in canter to a small jump staying straight through the guide poles. Remaining in canter make a square turn to the next jump.

Correct the canter lead if necessary on the short side of the arena and make a smooth turn to the next jump. Land straight and make another square turn to the next jump to finish.

Repeat in the opposite direction.

Aims:

- ✓ To encourage the rider to plan ahead
- ✓ To be accurate on the turns and focus on straightness
- ✓ To stop the horse from anticipating the direction
- ✓ To keep the same rhythm of canter throughout the exercise

Coach's tips:

- Support the horse with your inside leg to stop the horse from cutting the corner
- Use a half-halt to help rebalance the horse when necessary
- Look early for your line

Exercise 14 – Riding turn backs and square turns

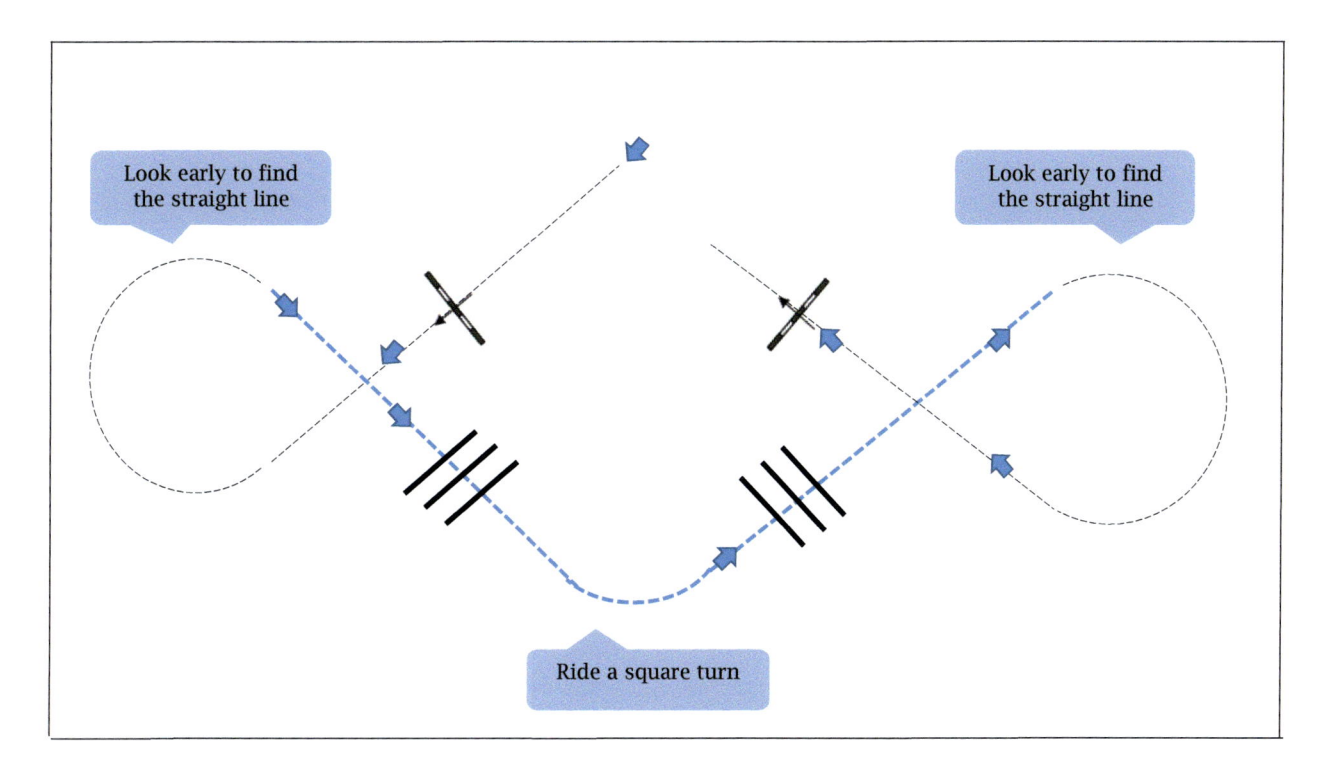

Diagram labels:
- Look early to find the straight line (left)
- Look early to find the straight line (right)
- Ride a square turn

Place two small jumps on a square turn and two sets of trotting poles on a square turn.

Start in canter to the small jump landing straight. Turn back on yourself and make a transition to trot in time for the trotting poles.
Make a square turn to the next set of trotting poles and then make a transition into canter and turn back on yourself to a small upright.

Repeat in the opposite direction to check the horse is even turning each way.

Aims:
- ✓ To encourage the rider to look early and plan ahead
- ✓ To develop straightness after a turn
- ✓ To improve transitions and encourage the horse to listen
- ✓ To increase rider/horse communication

Coach's tips:
- Use a half-halt to help rebalance the horse when necessary
- Look early for your line
- Be aware of the horse falling in or out on the turn back

Progression:
Move on to exercise 14a when the turns are smooth and the transitions are relaxed.

Exercise 14a - Riding turn backs and square turns

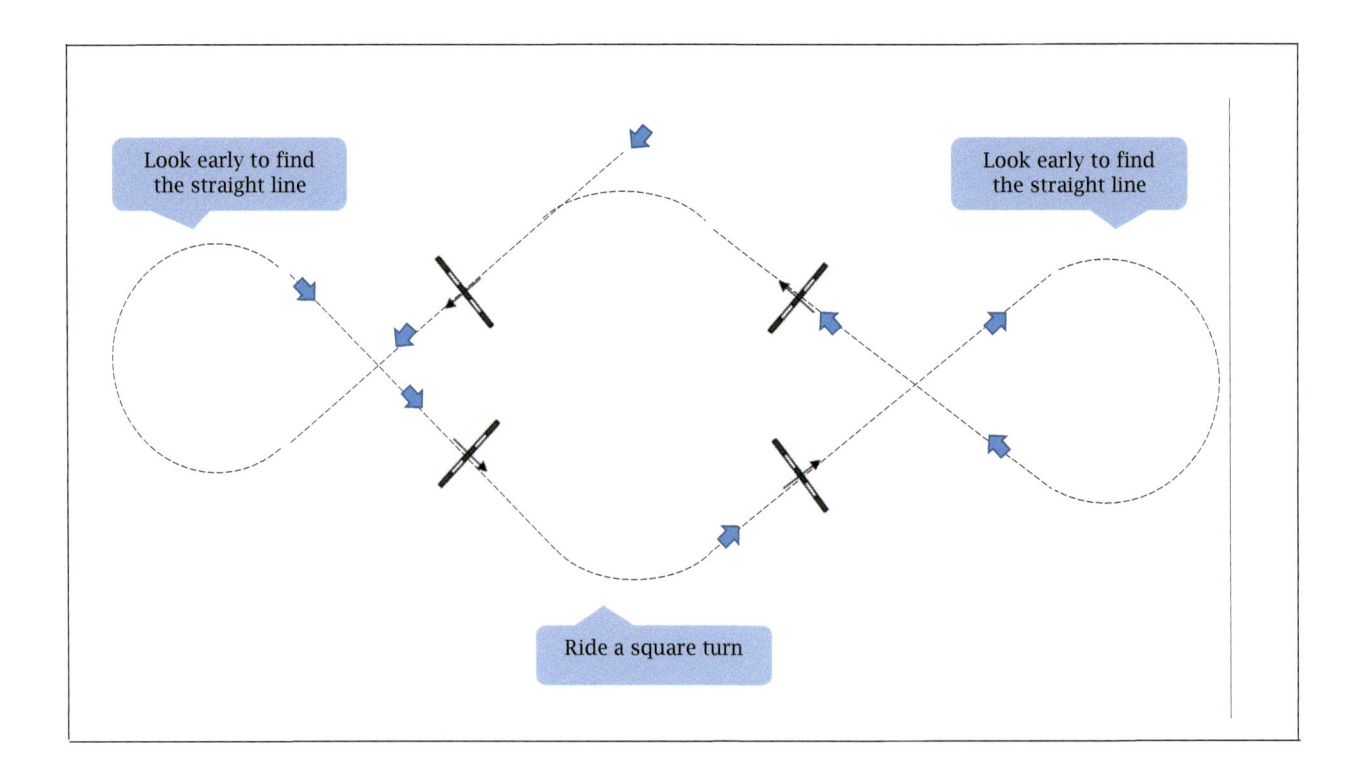

(Diagram labels: "Look early to find the straight line" — top left and top right; "Ride a square turn" — bottom centre)

Place four small jumps with square turns in the centre of the arena.

Start in canter to the first jump, landing straight. Make a smooth turn back on yourself and ride straight to the next jump.

Land straight and ride a square turn to the next jump, turning back on yourself to the last jump to finish.

Repeat in the opposite direction to check the horse is equally supple turning in both directions.

Aims:
- To encourage the rider to look early and plan ahead
- To improve balance and collection from the horse on landing
- To improve rider/horse communication
- To encourage the horse to listen

Coach's tips:
- Use a half-halt to help rebalance the horse when necessary
- Look early for your line and give clear instructions
- Be aware of the horse falling in or out on the turn back
- Give the horse time to think and learn

Exercise 15 – Riding angles

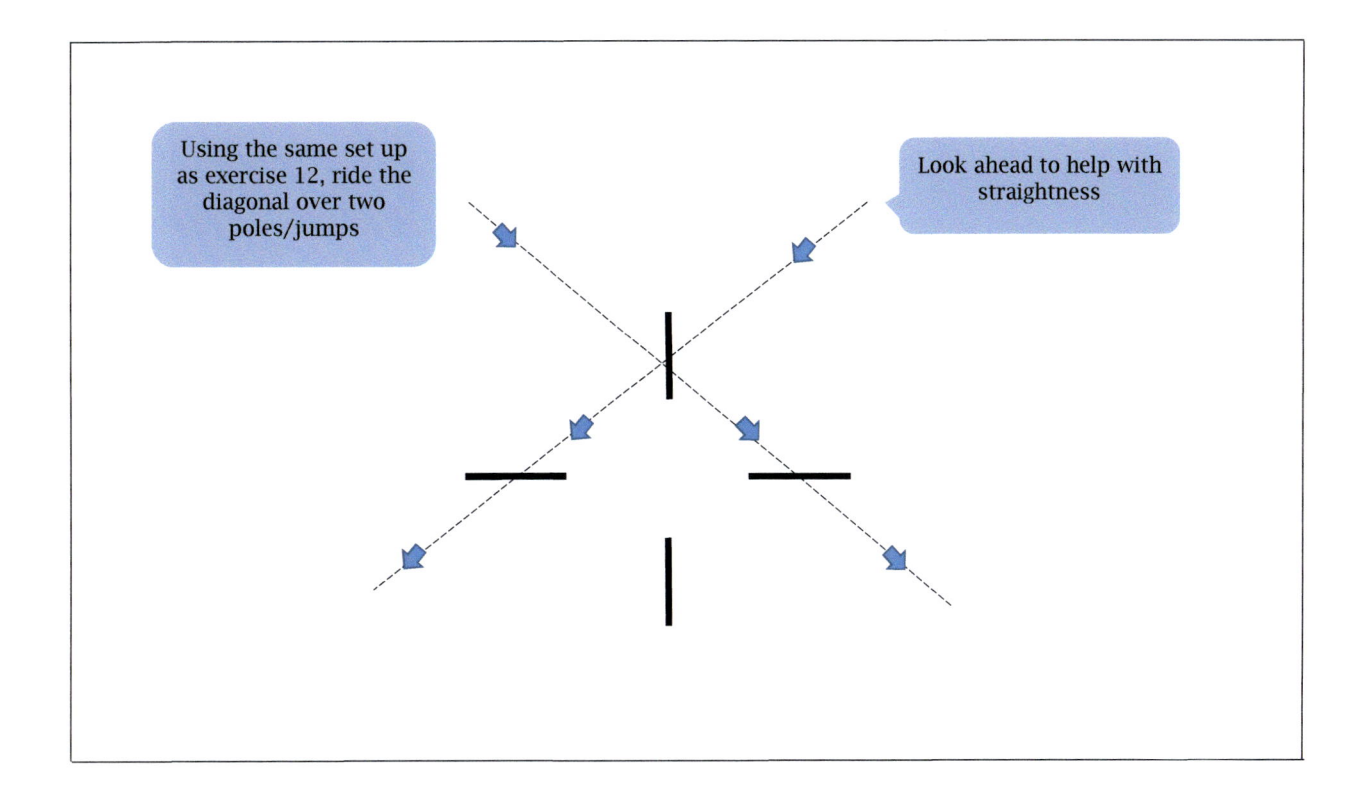

Using the same set up as exercise 12, ride the diagonal over two poles/jumps

Look ahead to help with straightness

Place four poles in a star shape in the centre of the arena with a gap of approx. 30ft (10 paces) between the inside ends of the poles.

Start this exercise in trot, until your horse is sure of the route, proceeding in canter when you feel ready.

Make sure you focus on the straight line by looking ahead. Find the line that works for your horse.

This exercise is good practice for the challenges in a jump-off.

Aims:
- ✓ To improve the rider's focus on straightness with poles facing different directions
- ✓ To develop forward planning
- ✓ To find the line that works for your horse's length of stride

Coach's tips:
- Keep the horse in a collected canter
- Make sure you look ahead and give the horse clear instructions
- Keep repeating to give your horse time to feel confident at angles

Progression:
To increase difficulty, change the poles into small jumps.

Exercise 15a - Riding angles

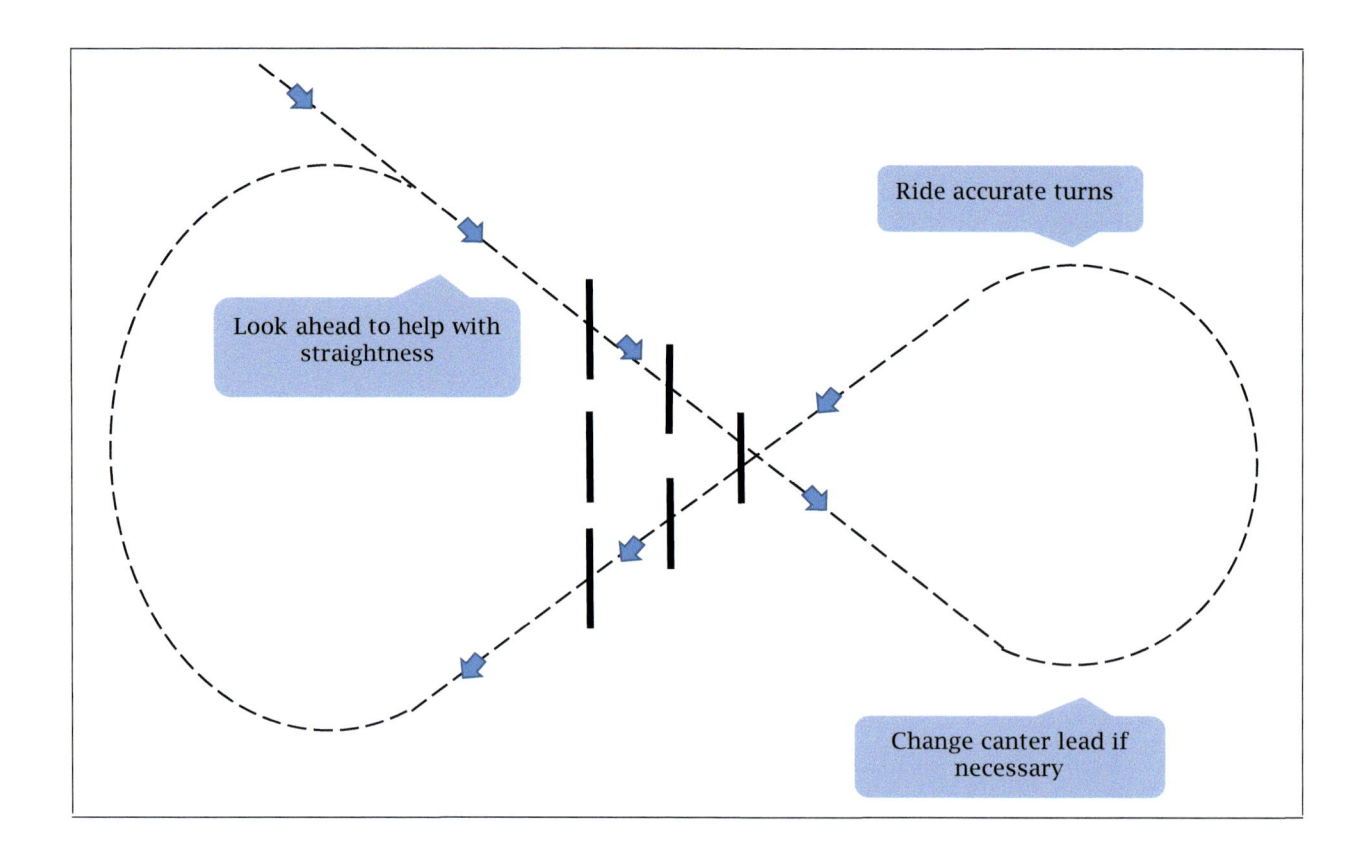

Diagram annotations:
- Look ahead to help with straightness
- Ride accurate turns
- Change canter lead if necessary

Place six poles in the centre of the arena in the shape of a pyramid (approx. 9ft apart)

Start this exercise in trot, until your horse is sure of the route, proceeding in canter when you feel ready.
Focus on the straight line by looking ahead.

Keep repeating to give your horse time to feel confident with the angles.

This exercise is good practice for the challenges in a jump-off.

Aims:

- ✓ To improve the rider's focus on straightness with poles at an angle
- ✓ To develop forward planning
- ✓ To encourage the rider to look early from the turn

Coach's tips:

- Keep the horse in a collected canter
- Make sure you look ahead and give the horse clear instructions
- Find the line that works for your horse and give the horse chance to think for himself

Exercise 15b – Riding angles

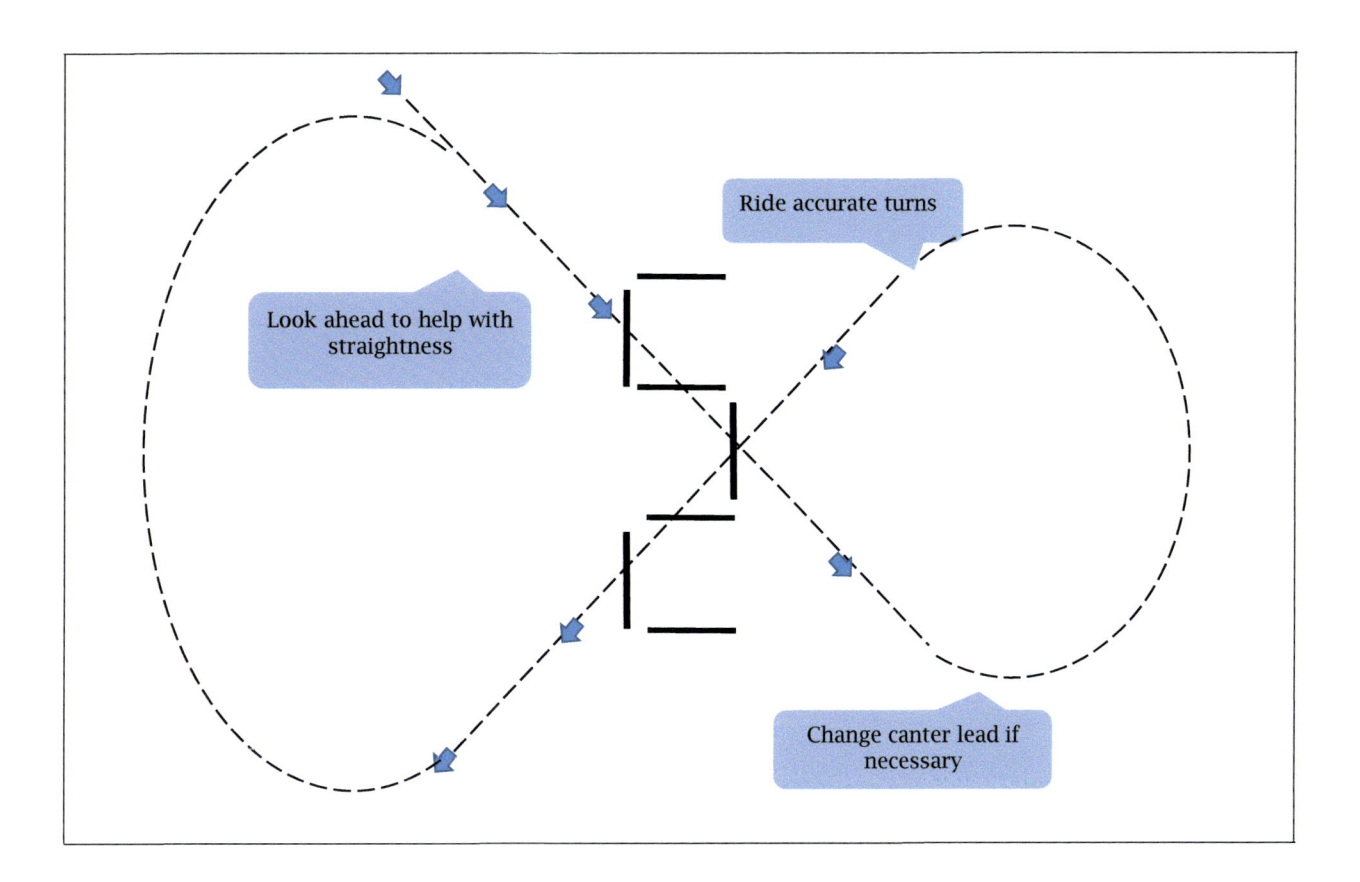

Diagram labels:
- Look ahead to help with straightness
- Ride accurate turns
- Change canter lead if necessary

Place seven poles in the centre of the arena as shown above.

Start this exercise in trot, until your horse is sure of the route, proceeding in canter when appropriate.

Make sure you focus on the straight line by looking ahead.
Keep repeating to give your horse time to feel confident with angles.

This exercise is good practice for the challenges you might meet in a jump-off.

Aims:
- ✓ To improve the rider's focus on straightness with poles at different angles
- ✓ To develop forward planning
- ✓ To encourage the rider to look early from the turn

Coach's tips:
- Keep your body weight central to help with the balance and straightness
- Make sure you look ahead and give the horse clear instructions
- Find the line that works for your horse, and repeat to give your horse chance to learn

Exercise 16 – Riding angles within a course

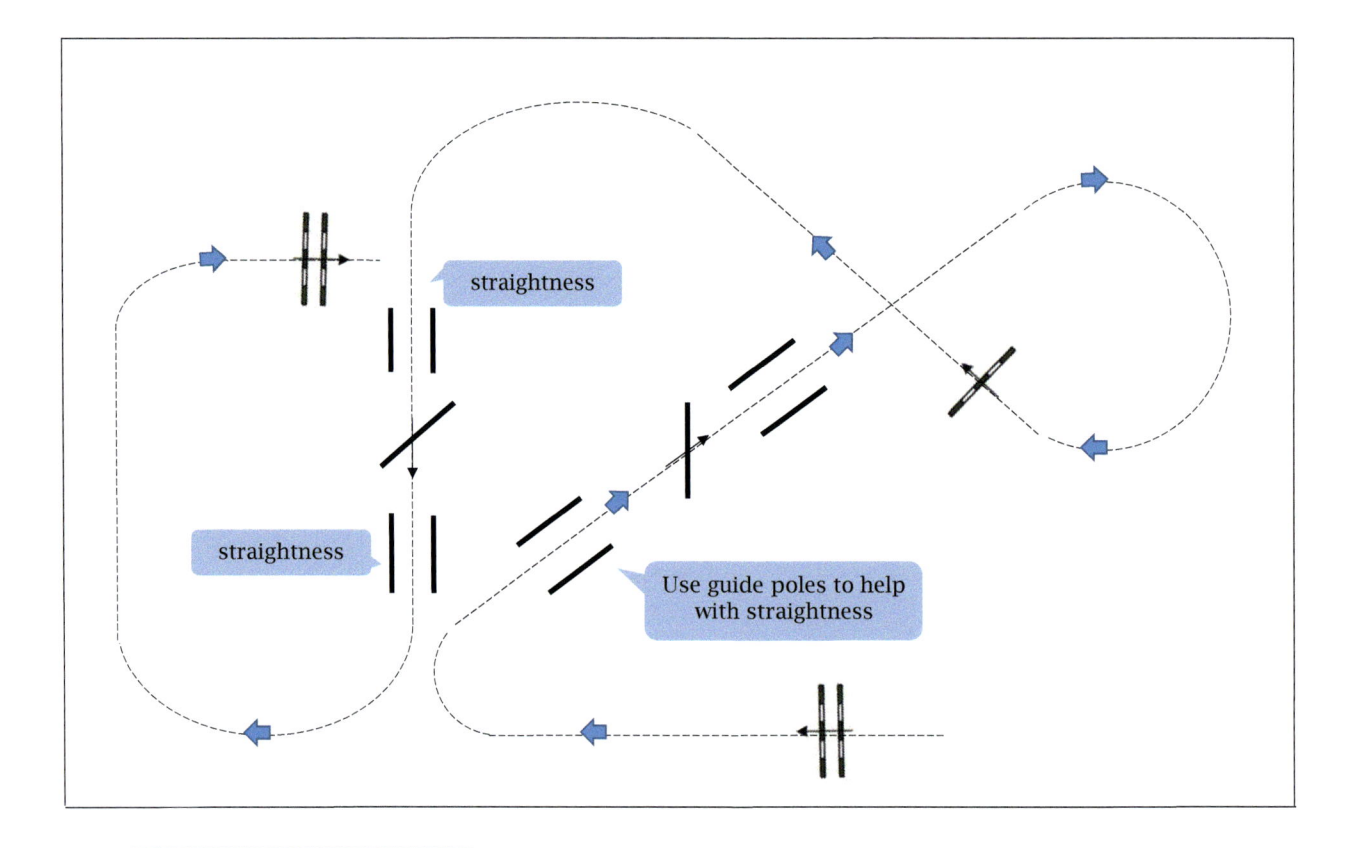

Diagram labels: straightness; straightness; Use guide poles to help with straightness

Use the arena set up illustrated above to prepare for jump-off lines.

Start on a straight line to the first jump before turning right and jumping a jump across the angle. Make a turn back on yourself to the next jump and then ride a left turn to the next jump which should be positioned on an angle. Finish by turning right to the last jump.

Repeat in the opposite directions to keep your work equal on both reins.

Aims:
- ✓ To prepare both the rider and horse for challenges they might meet in a jump-off
- ✓ To improve rider/horse communication
- ✓ To encourage the rider to plan ahead throughout the course

Coach's tips:
- Look early for your line and give clear instructions
- Be aware of the horse falling in or out on the turns
- Keep thinking 'one jump ahead'

Progression:
When the horse feels confident, make your turns a little tighter.

Exercise 17 - Planning ahead for multiple angles

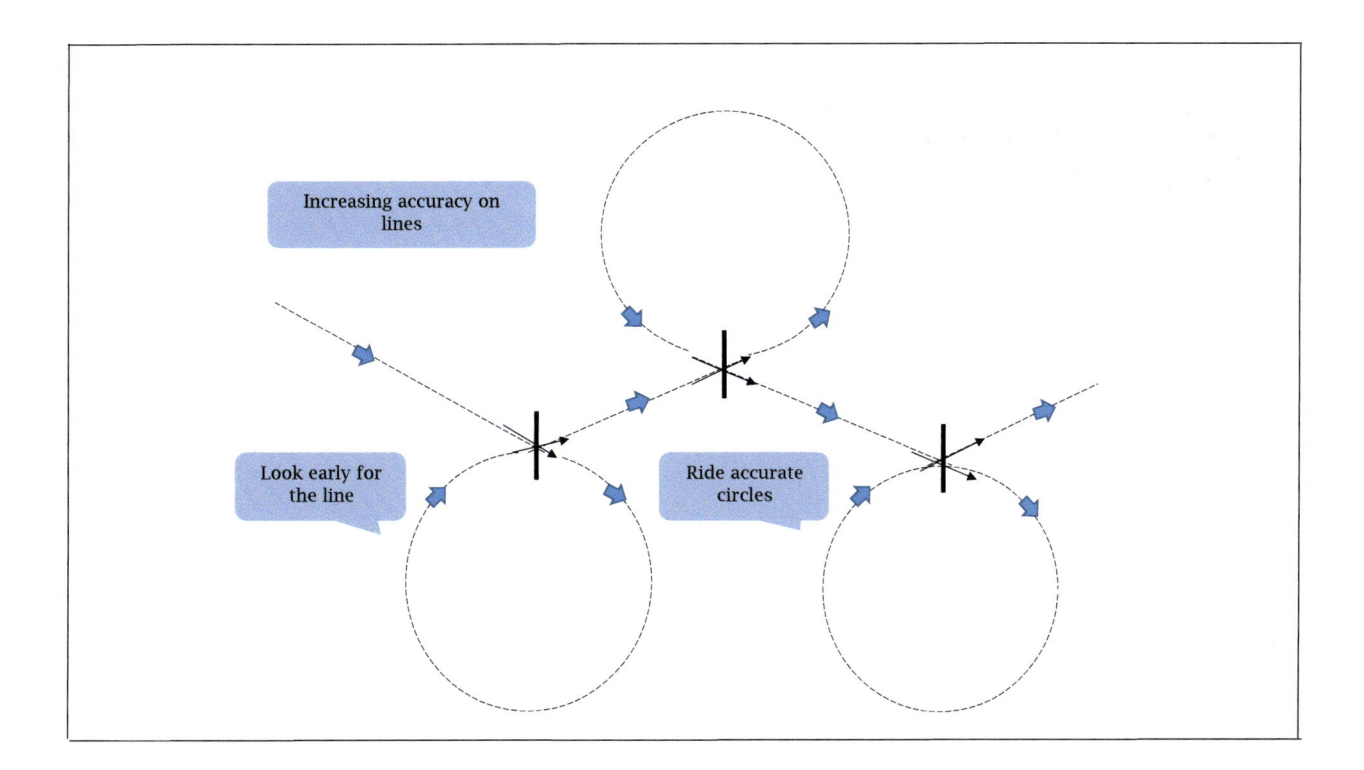

Diagram labels: Increasing accuracy on lines; Look early for the line; Ride accurate circles

Place three poles (3 or 4 canter strides apart) on a staggered line in the centre of the arena.

Start by cantering to the first pole on an angle and circle to the right, returning to the pole on the opposite angle. Ride straight on the angle to the next pole, circling left and returning to the pole. Ride straight over the last pole, circle right and returning to the final pole to finish.

Repeat from the opposite direction, keeping your work equal on both reins.

Aims:

- ✓ To prepare both the rider and horse for challenges they might meet in a jump-off
- ✓ To improve rider/horse communication
- ✓ To encourage the rider to look forward and plan ahead

Coach's tips:

- Look early for your line and give clear instructions
- Be aware of the horse wobbling off the straight line and support with even rein contact and even weight in both stirrups

Exercise 17a - Planning ahead for alternate angles

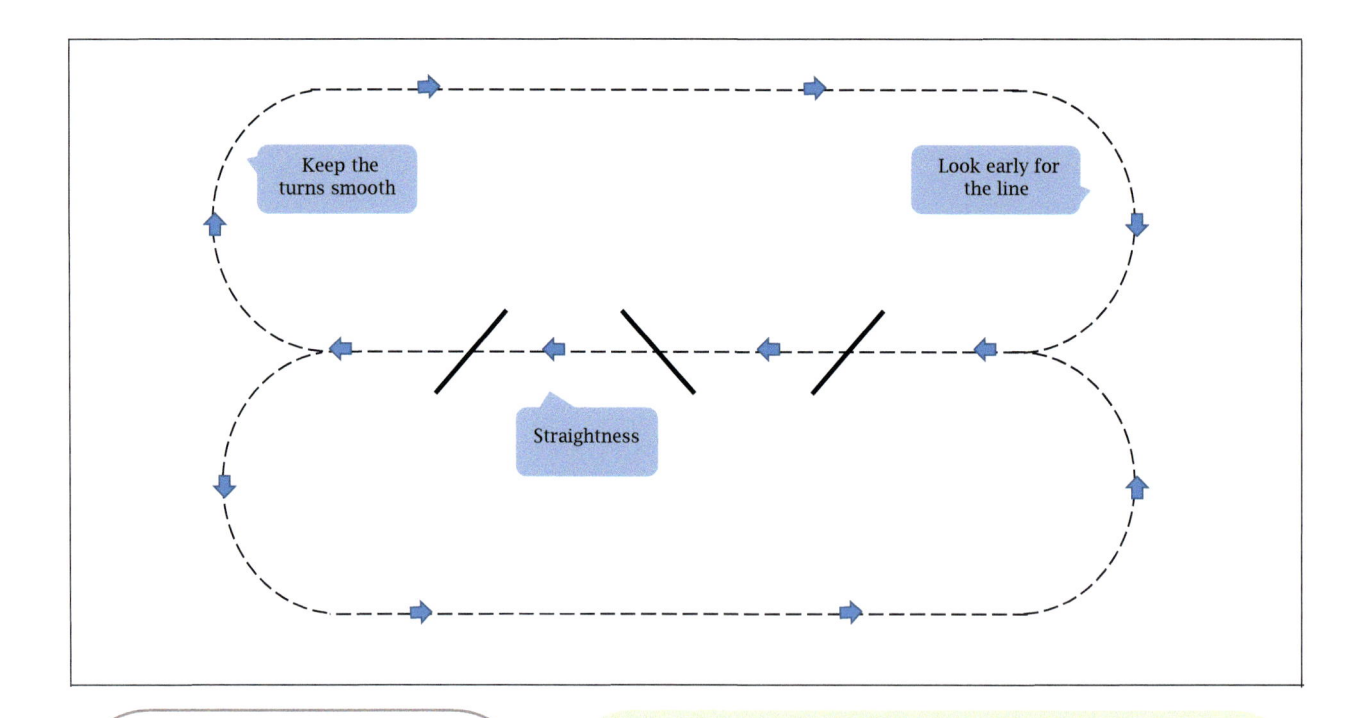

Diagram labels: "Keep the turns smooth", "Look early for the line", "Straightness"

Place three poles on the centre of the arena at alternate angles (3 or 4 canter strides apart).

Start by cantering on the right rein down the centre line, focussing on staying straight.
Turn left at the end of the arena and ride the exercise again from the left turn.
Keep alternating the direction of turn.

Repeat from the opposite direction to keep your work equal on both reins.

Aims:

- ✓ To improve rider/horse communication
- ✓ To encourage the rider to look forward and plan ahead
- ✓ To be more focused on the line and not be distracted by the angle of the pole/jump

Coach's tips:

- Look early for your line and give clear instructions
- Be aware of the straight line, but give your horse time to work it out
- Keep your body central and in balance to help with straightness

Progression:
When your horse is confident with the route, change the poles into small jumps.

Exercise 17b – Planning ahead for alternate angles

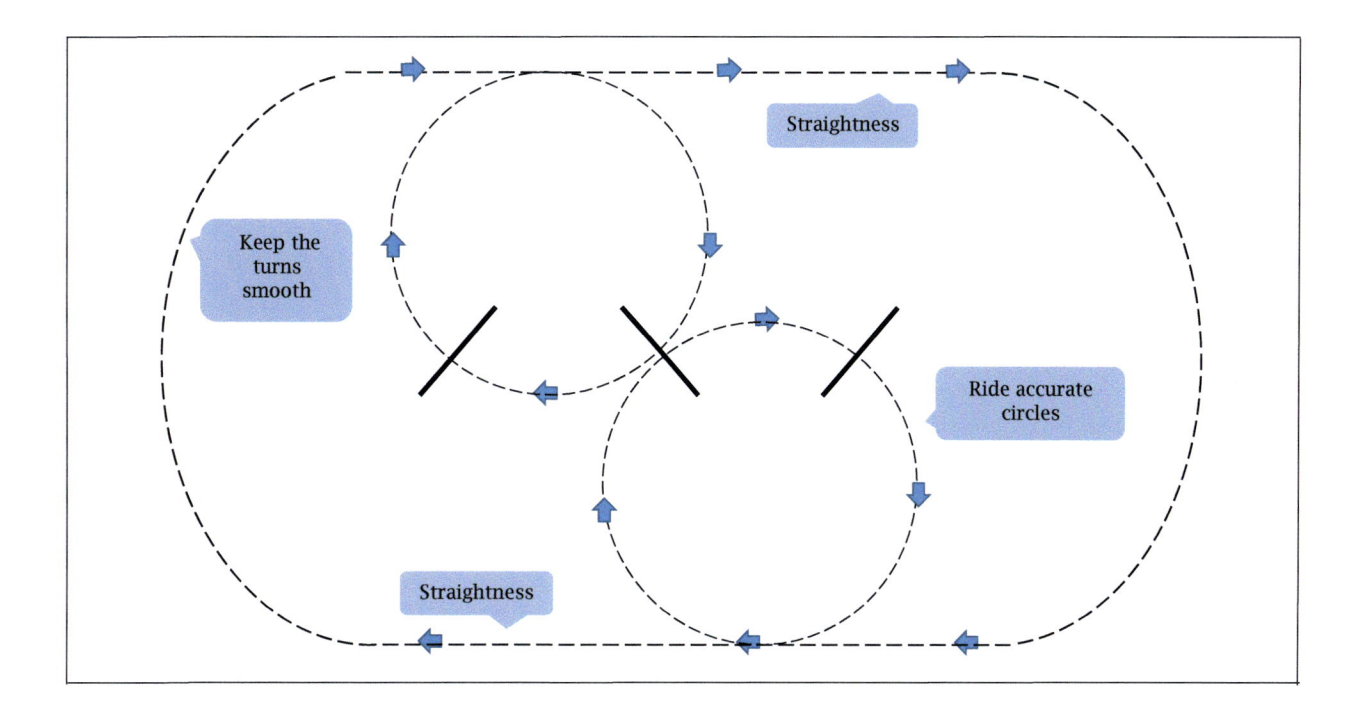

Diagram labels: Keep the turns smooth; Straightness; Ride accurate circles; Straightness

Place three poles on the centre of the arena at alternate angles (3 canter strides apart).

Start by cantering on the right rein on the long side making a circle that incorporates the first two poles.
Exit the circle and go large around the arena before circling over the first two poles from the opposite side of the arena.

Repeat on both reins, to keep your work consistent.

Aims:

- ✓ To improve rider/ horse communication
- ✓ To encourage the rider to look forward and plan ahead
- ✓ To be more focused on the circles and not be distracted by the angle of the pole/jump

Coach's tips:

- Look early for your line and give clear instructions
- Be aware of the horse falling in or out on the circle
- Make sure your hips and shoulders are parallel to the pole/jump at all times

Progression:
When your horse is confident with the route, change the poles into small jumps.

Exercise 18 – Alternating the turn backs with transitions

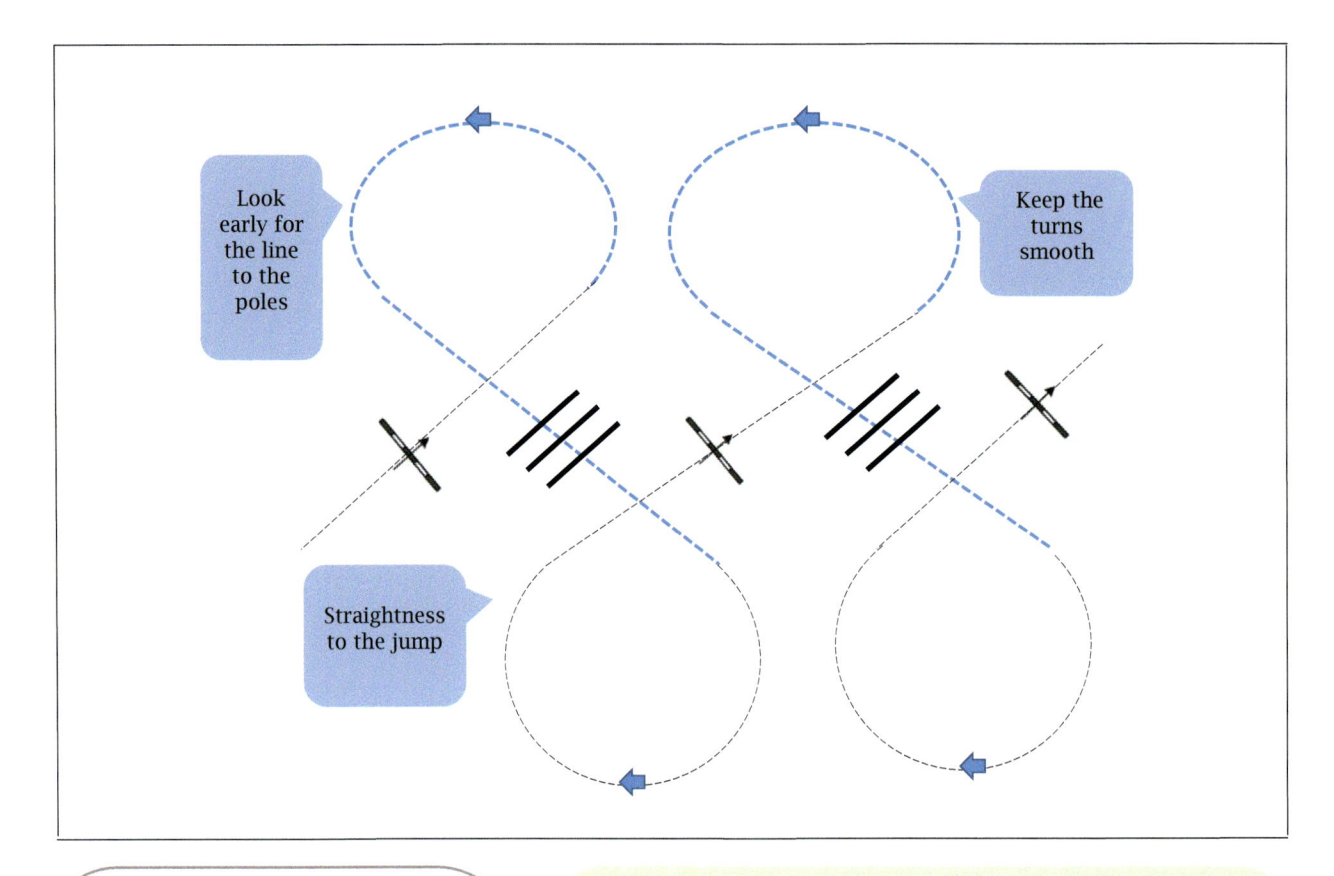

Look early for the line to the poles

Keep the turns smooth

Straightness to the jump

Place three small jumps and two sets of trotting poles down the centre line, alternating the direction of each.
Start in canter to the first small jump, staying straight on landing. Make a transition to trot before turning back in a loop to the left and straight to the trotting poles.
Make a transition into canter before riding a loop to the right and straight to the next upright.
Complete the exercise using the same format.
Repeat the exercise in the opposite direction.

Aims:

- ✓ To make smooth transitions
- ✓ To look early for the line
- ✓ To encourage the rider to plan ahead for the route
- ✓ To keep the horse listening

Coach's tips:

- Make sure you are straight before and after the poles/jumps
- Be aware of the horse falling in or out on the turn
- Ride bigger loops if the horse is finding it a challenge, or smaller if it is too easy

Progression:
To increase difficulty, move on to exercise 18a.

Exercise 18a - Alternating the turn backs

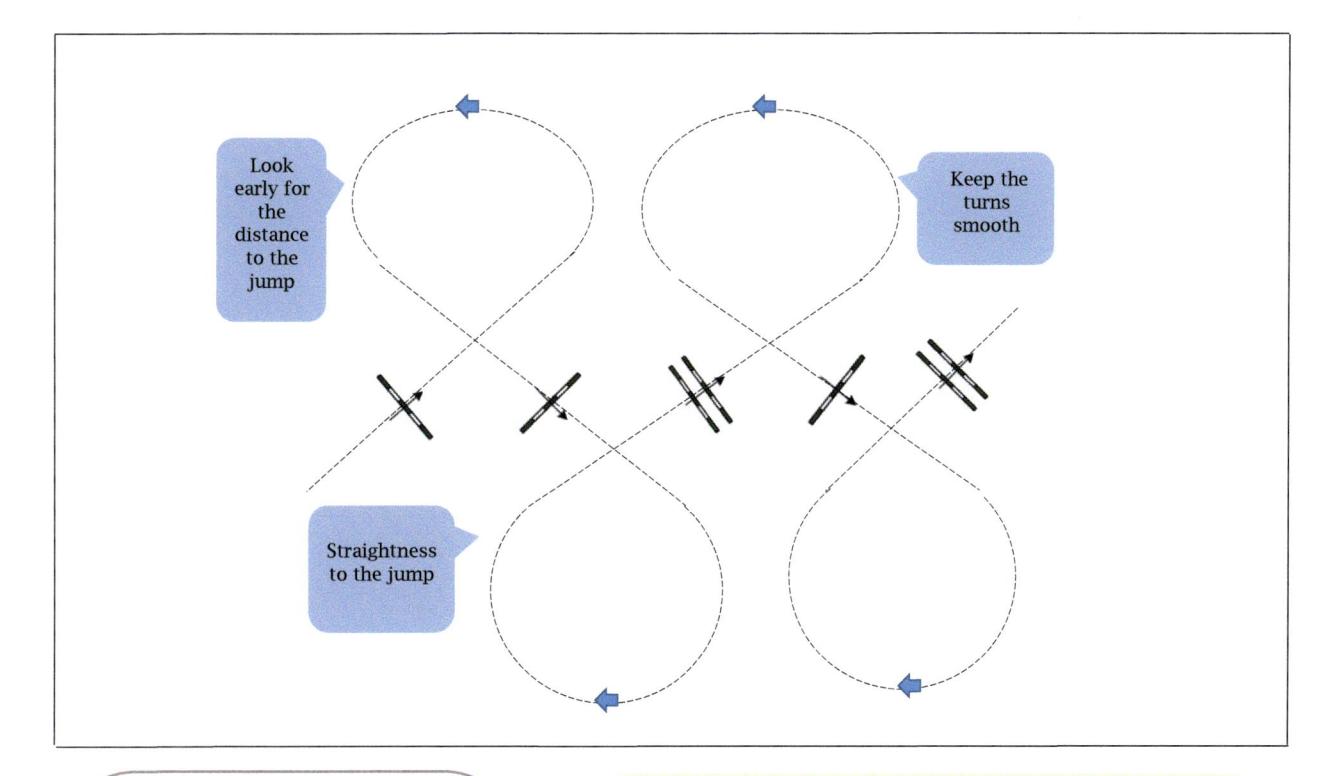

Diagram labels:
- Look early for the distance to the jump
- Keep the turns smooth
- Straightness to the jump

Place five small jumps down the centre line, alternating the direction of each.

Start in canter to the first small jump, staying straight on landing. Make a change of lead (if necessary) before turning back in a loop to the left and straight to the next jump. Ride straight before riding a loop to the right to the next jump. Complete the exercise using the same format.

Repeat the exercise from the opposite direction.

Aims:
- ✓ To keep the rhythm and balance in the canter on the turn backs
- ✓ To look early for the distance to the jump
- ✓ To use subtle body language to influence the correct lead on landing

Coach's tips:
- Be aware of your horse falling in or out on the circle
- Make sure your shoulders and hips are parallel to the jumps at all times
- Be ready for your horse to anticipate the direction of the turn

Progression:
For further work on accurate turns, move on to exercise 19.

Exercise 19 – Preparing for jump-off turns

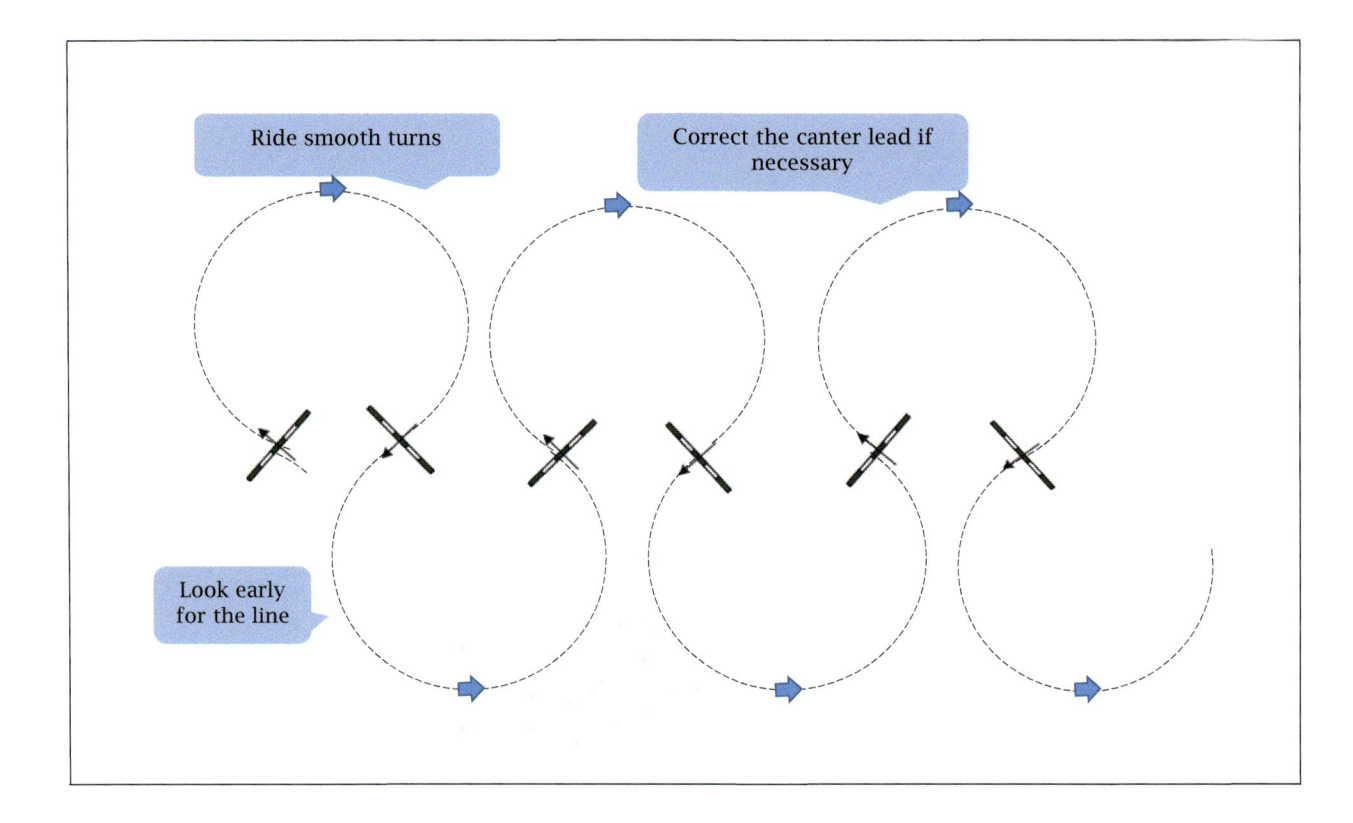

Diagram labels:
- Ride smooth turns
- Correct the canter lead if necessary
- Look early for the line

Place six small jumps on the centre line at alternate angles.

Start in canter and ride straight to the first jump making a smooth turn to the right to the next jump, ensuring straightness on take-off and landing. Ride another smooth turn to the left to the next jump, again making sure of the straightness on take-off and landing. Complete the exercise following the same format.

Repeat the exercise from the opposite direction.

Aims:

- ✓ To encourage the rider to look early and plan ahead
- ✓ To use subtle body language to influence the correct lead on landing
- ✓ To improve rider/horse communication
- ✓ To keep the rhythm of canter

Coach's tips:

- Keep 'on the boil' and give clear instructions
- Be aware of the horse falling in or out on the turns
- Be ready for your horse to anticipate the direction of the turn

Exercise 20 – Preparing for jump-offs

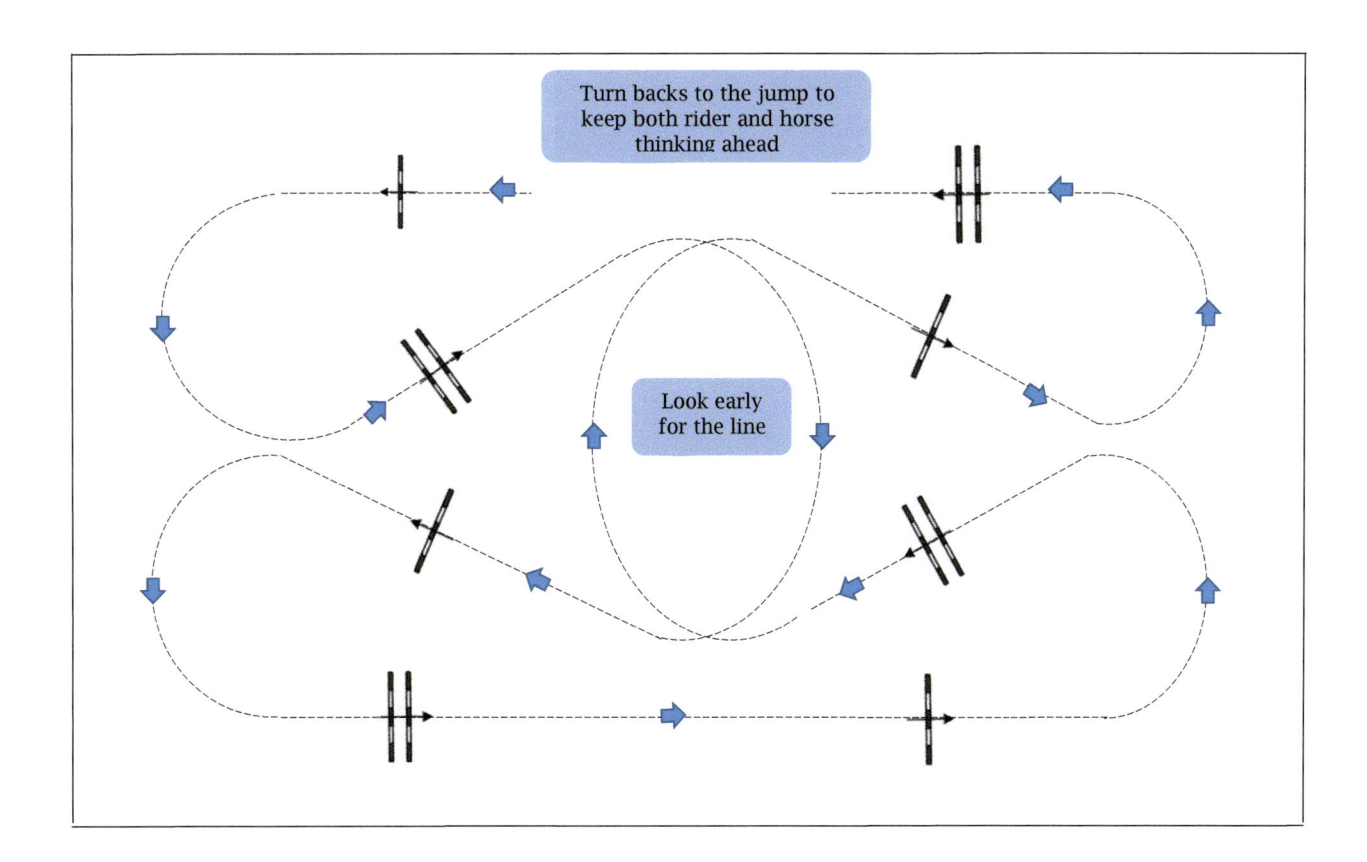

Diagram labels:
- Turn backs to the jump to keep both rider and horse thinking ahead
- Look early for the line

Use the course set up as illustrated, to practice your turns for jump-offs.

Start by riding straight to the first jump and make alternate turns after each jump.

To increase difficulty, make the turns a little tighter.

This course can be repeated in reverse.

Aims:
- ✓ To encourage the rider to look early and plan ahead
- ✓ To use subtle body language to influence the correct lead on landing
- ✓ Improve rider/horse communication
- ✓ To keep the rhythm of canter over a longer course

Coach's tips:
- Make sure your shoulders and hips are parallel to the jumps at all times
- Be aware of the horse falling in or out on the turn
- Always think 'one jump ahead'

Exercise 21 - Riding the bending line

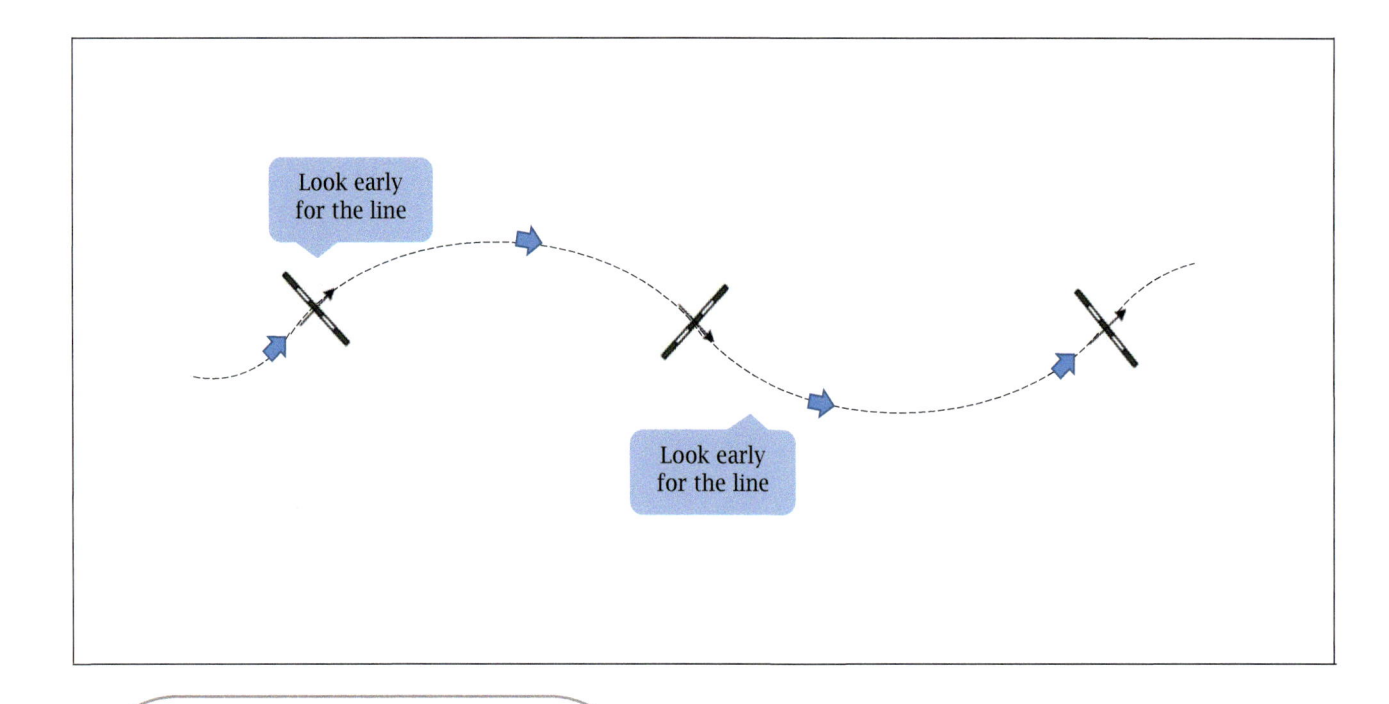

Look early for the line

Look early for the line

Place three small jumps on a zigzag down the centre line of the arena.

Start in canter on the left rein to the first jump and then follow the curve to the right over the next jump.
Land straight and follow the curve to the left to the last jump.

Repeat from the opposite direction.

This exercise works equally well using poles rather than jumps.

Aims:
- ✓ To encourage the rider to plan ahead
- ✓ To improve control on the bending line
- ✓ To increase the rider's focus for the next two jumps and not just the jump in front of them

Coach's tips:
- Remember to bend the horse around your inside leg on the curve, using your outside rein to help maintain straightness for the jump
- Keep focussing forward

Progression:
Move on to exercise 21a when your horse is ready.

Exercise 21a - Riding the bending line

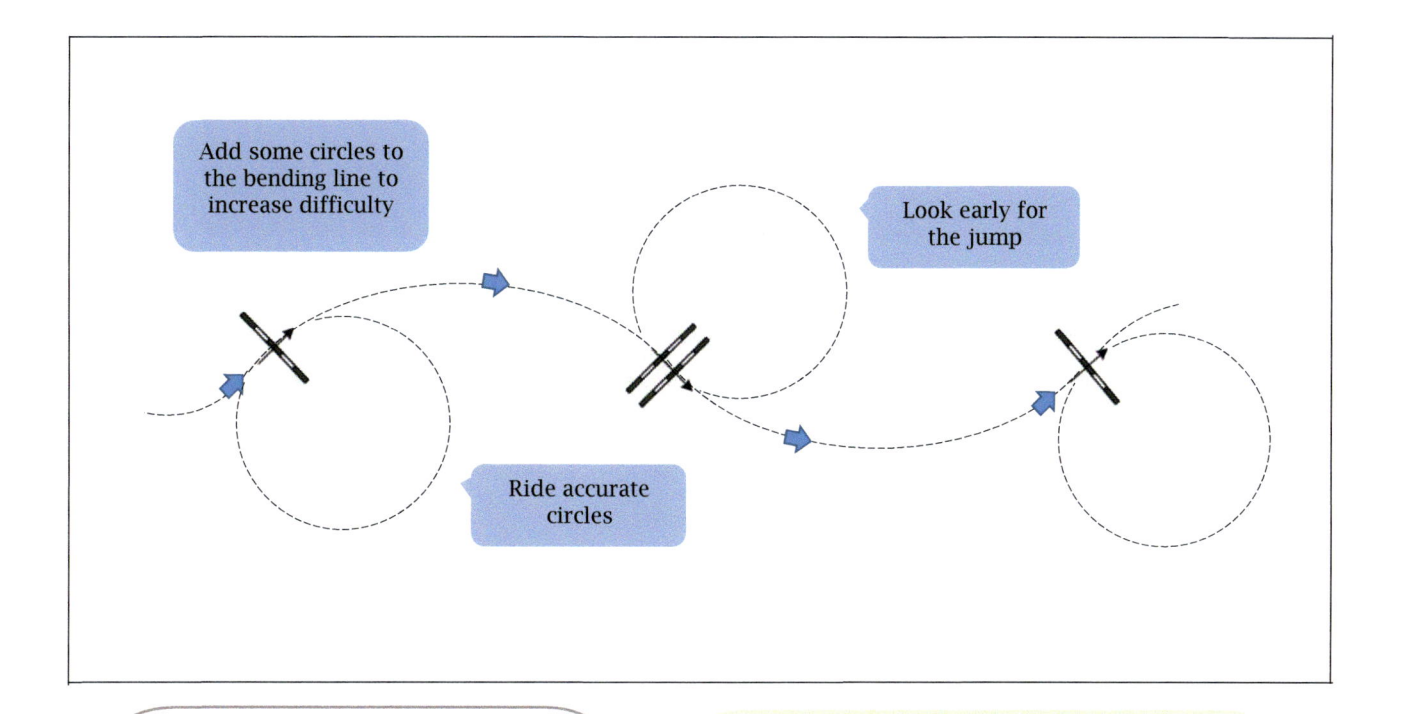

Diagram annotations:
- Add some circles to the bending line to increase difficulty
- Look early for the jump
- Ride accurate circles

Place three small jumps on a zigzag down the centre line of the arena.

Start in canter on the left rein to the first jump circling to the right on landing, jumping the jump again. Then follow the curve to the right to the next jump. Circle to the left on landing and follow the curve to the left to the last jump. Circle to the right on landing and jump the jump again to finish.

Repeat from the opposite direction.

This exercise works equally well with just poles.

Aims:
- ✓ To encourage the rider to plan ahead
- ✓ To improve control on the bending line
- ✓ To stop the horse anticipating the line
- ✓ To improve rider/horse communication

Coach's tips:
- Be aware of the horse falling in or out on the circles
- Make sure your hips and shoulders are parallel to the jump at all times

Progression:
Move on to exercise 21b when your horse is ready.

Exercise 21b - Riding the bending line

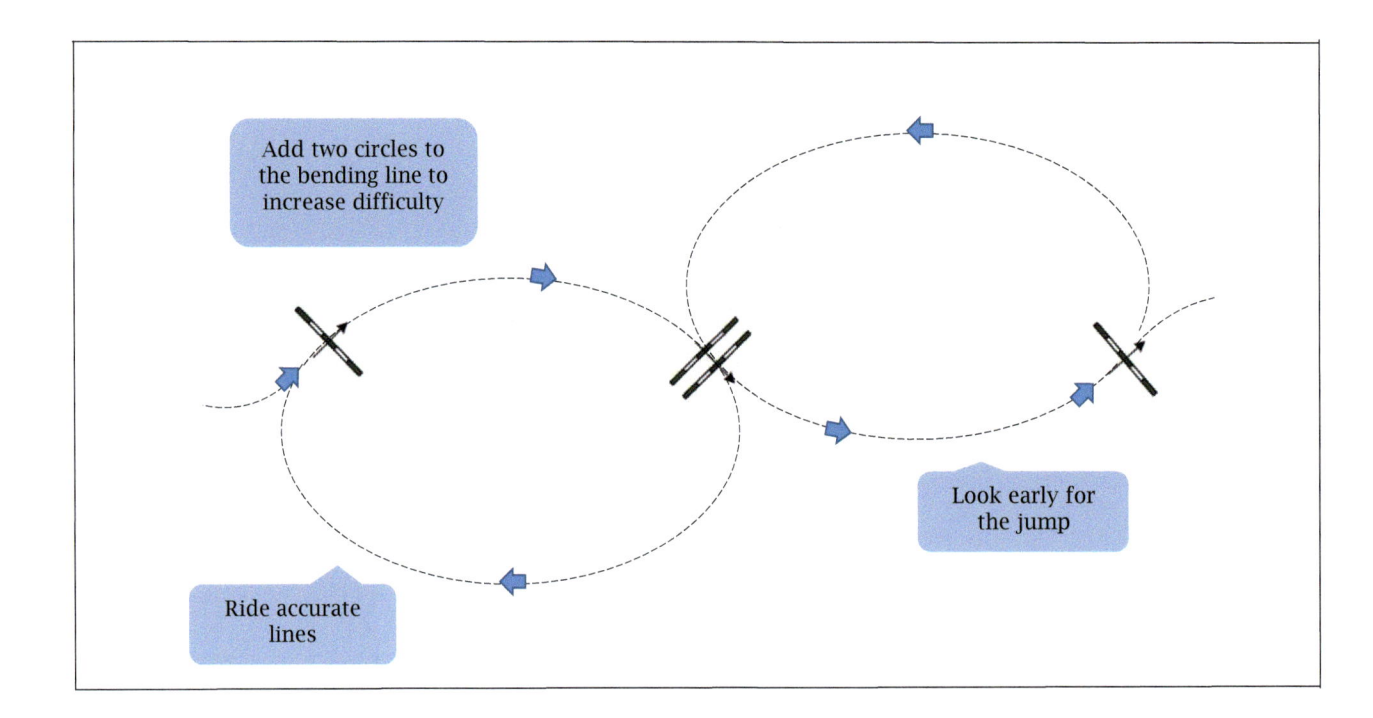

Diagram labels:
- Add two circles to the bending line to increase difficulty
- Look early for the jump
- Ride accurate lines

Place three small jumps on a zigzag down the centre line of the arena.

Increase the difficulty of exercise 21a.

Start in canter on the left rein, complete the first two jumps, circle to the right on landing, jump both jumps again. Follow the curve to the left jumping the next jump, circling left on landing and jumping the last two jumps again to finish.

Repeat from the opposite direction.

This exercise works equally well with just poles.

Aims:

- ✓ To encourage the rider to plan ahead
- ✓ To stop the horse anticipating the line
- ✓ To improve rider/horse communication and listening

Coach's tips:

- Be clear with your instructions
- Make sure your hips and shoulders are parallel to the jump at all times
- Take your time, don't let the exercise feel rushed

Exercise 22 - Turning back to the straight line

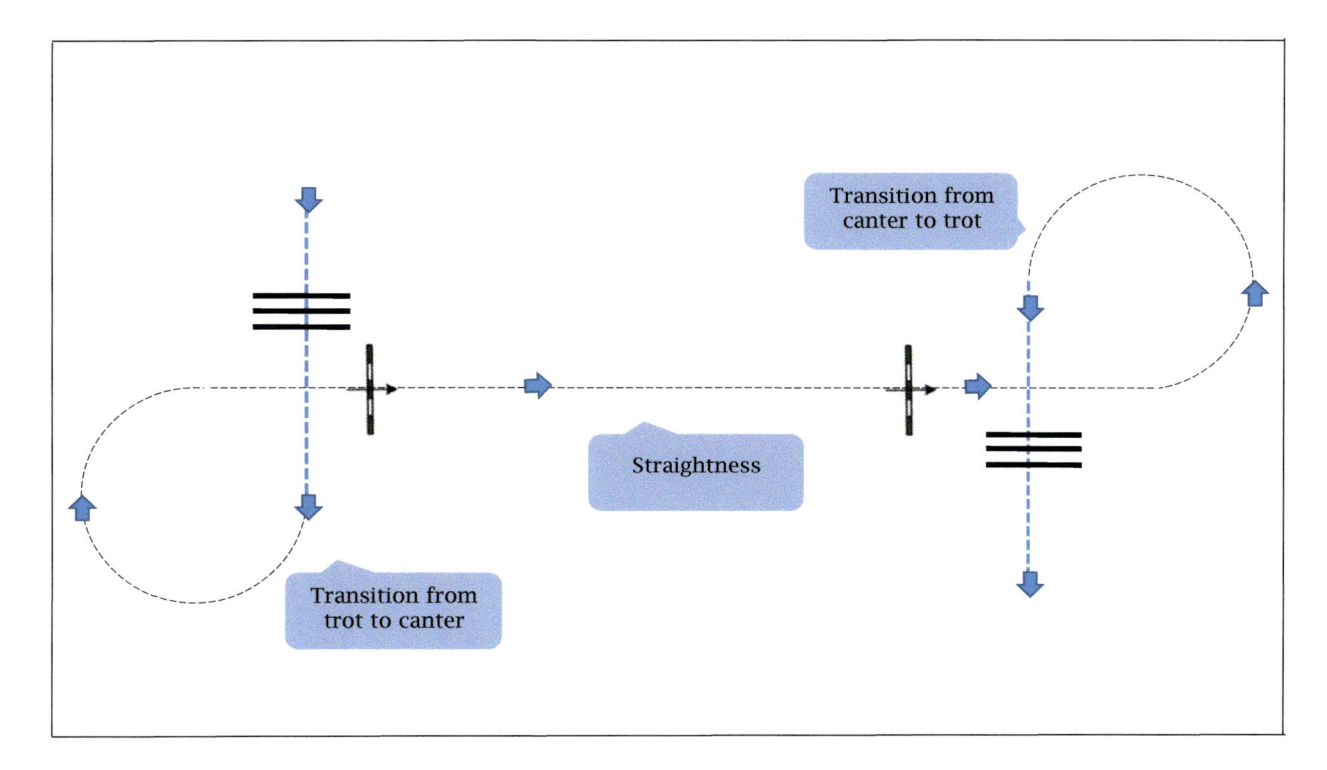

Diagram labels: Transition from canter to trot; Straightness; Transition from trot to canter

Place two small jumps on the centre line of the arena. Then place two sets of trotting poles at 90 degrees to the two jumps, as shown above.

Start in trot across the arena to the trotting poles. Make a right turn and a transition into canter before turning down the centre line and completing both jumps.
At the end of the arena make a left turn and a transition to trot before becoming straight for the trotting poles.

Repeat from the opposite direction.

Aims:

- ✓ To focus on straightness, smooth turns and transitions
- ✓ To encourage the rider to plan ahead
- ✓ To make sure the horse is relaxed at the beginning and the end of the exercise

Coach's tips:

- Make your turn back bigger initially to allow time for a smooth transition
- Look early to find the centre line
- Transitions must not feel forced, give your horse time to think and learn

Progression:
Move on to exercise 22a when you are ready.

Exercise 22a - Turning back to the straight line

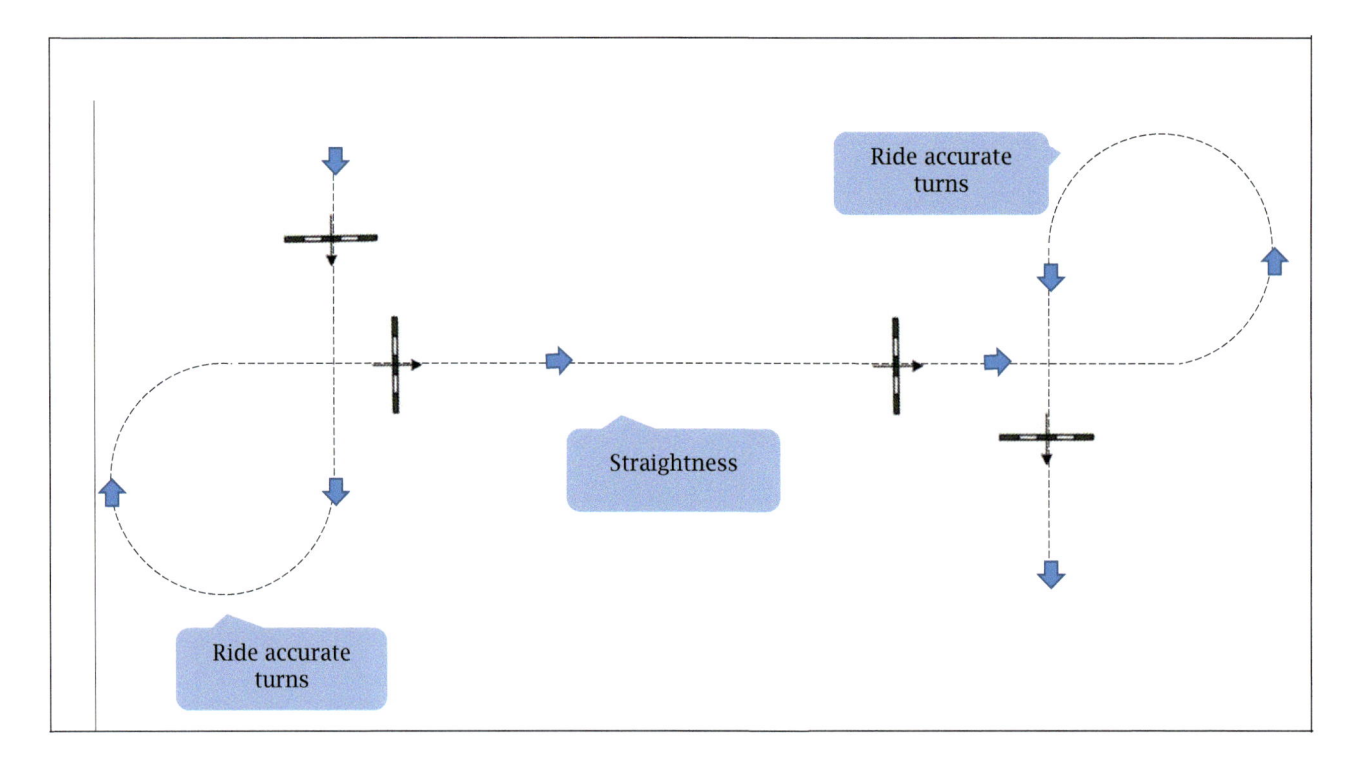

Place two small jumps on the centre line of the arena. Then place two more jumps at 90 degrees to the first two jumps as shown above.

Start in canter across the arena to the first jump. Make a right turn, changing the canter lead if necessary, before turning down the centre line to the next two jumps.
At the end of the arena make a left turn, changing the canter lead if required, before turning back to the last jump.

Repeat from the opposite direction.

Aims:
- ✓ To focus on straightness and smooth turns
- ✓ To encourage the rider to plan ahead
- ✓ To make sure the horse is equally supple on both reins when turning back to the jumps

Coach's tips:
- Make sure you bend the horse around your inside leg on the turns
- Use your outside rein to create straightness for the jump
- Look early to find the centre line

Progression:
Make your turn backs tighter to increase difficulty.

Exercise 23 – Engaging the canter and accurate lines

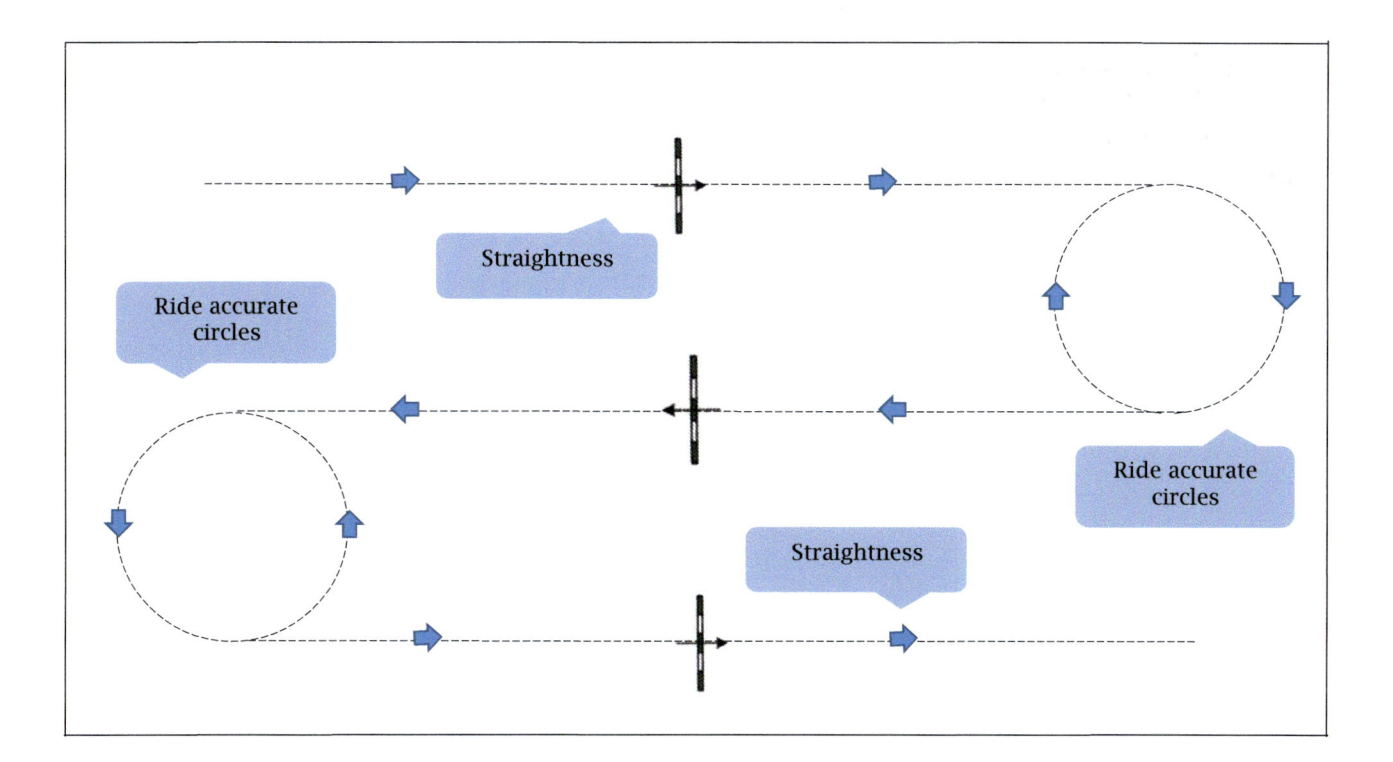

Place three small jumps across the centre line as shown above.

Starting on the right rein, canter a straight line to the first jump. At the end of the arena make a small circle to the right before turning down the centre line to the next jump.
At the end of the arena make a small circle to the left before continuing straight to the last jump, staying straight to finish.

Repeat from the opposite direction.

Aims:
- ✓ To increase rider accuracy of turns and straightness
- ✓ To improve collection and quality of canter
- ✓ To keep the rider planning ahead

Coach's tips:
- Remember to use a half-halt to balance the horse before the small circles
- Be aware of the horse falling in or out on the circle
- Use the circles to encourage the horse to relax

Progression:
Move on to exercise 23a when your horse is ready.

Exercise 23a – Engaging the canter and accurate lines

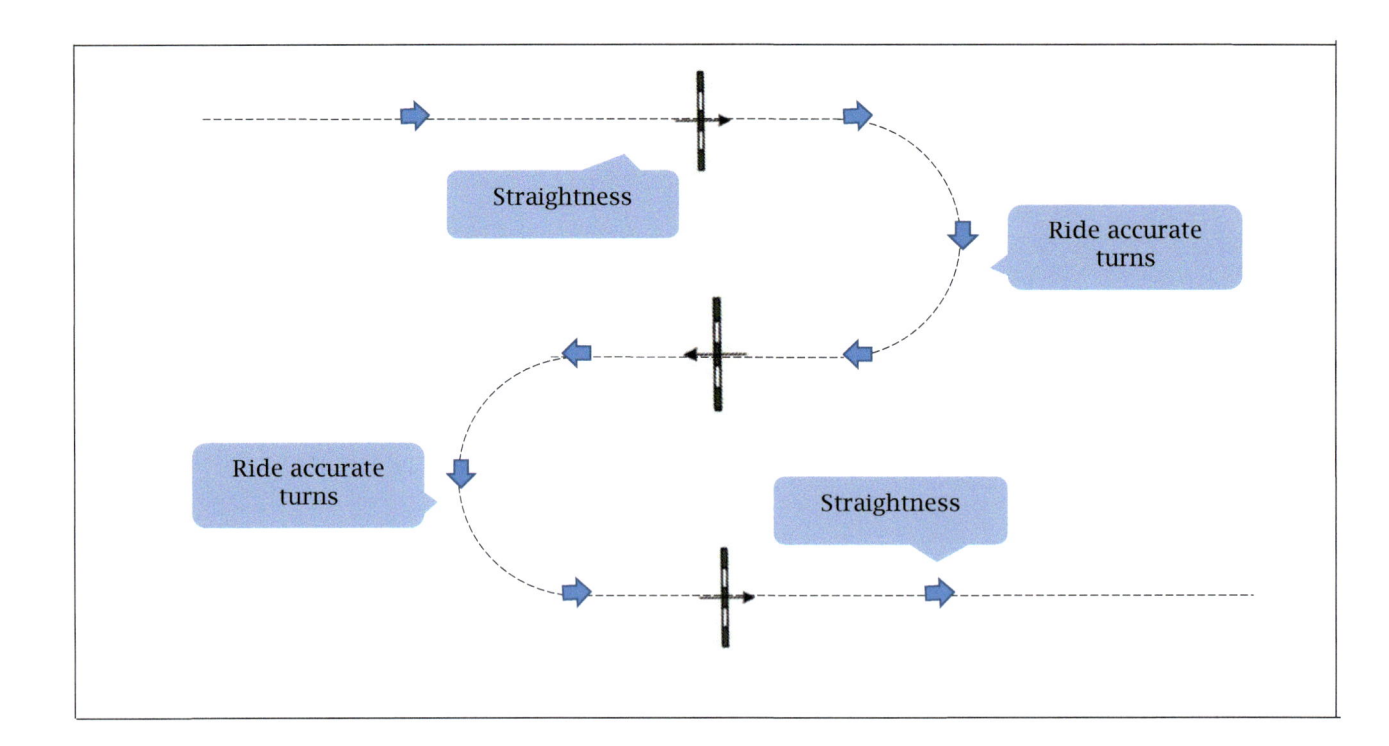

Diagram: Three small jumps placed across the centre line with a serpentine path showing "Straightness" on the straight approaches and "Ride accurate turns" on the curved sections.

Place three small jumps across the centre line as shown above.

Starting on the right rein, canter a straight line to the first jump and then turn right down the centre line to the next jump. Make sure you are straight before you turn left to the last jump, staying straight to finish.

Repeat from the opposite direction.

Aims:
- To increase rider accuracy of turns and straightness
- To improve collection and quality of canter
- To keep the rider planning ahead
- To encourage the horse to listen

Coach's tips:
- Remember to use a half-halt to balance the horse before the turns
- Look early to the jump, always think one jump ahead
- Make sure your hips and shoulders are parallel to the jump

Progression;
When your horse feels ready, make your turns tighter to increase the difficulty.

Exercise 24 – Riding with precision

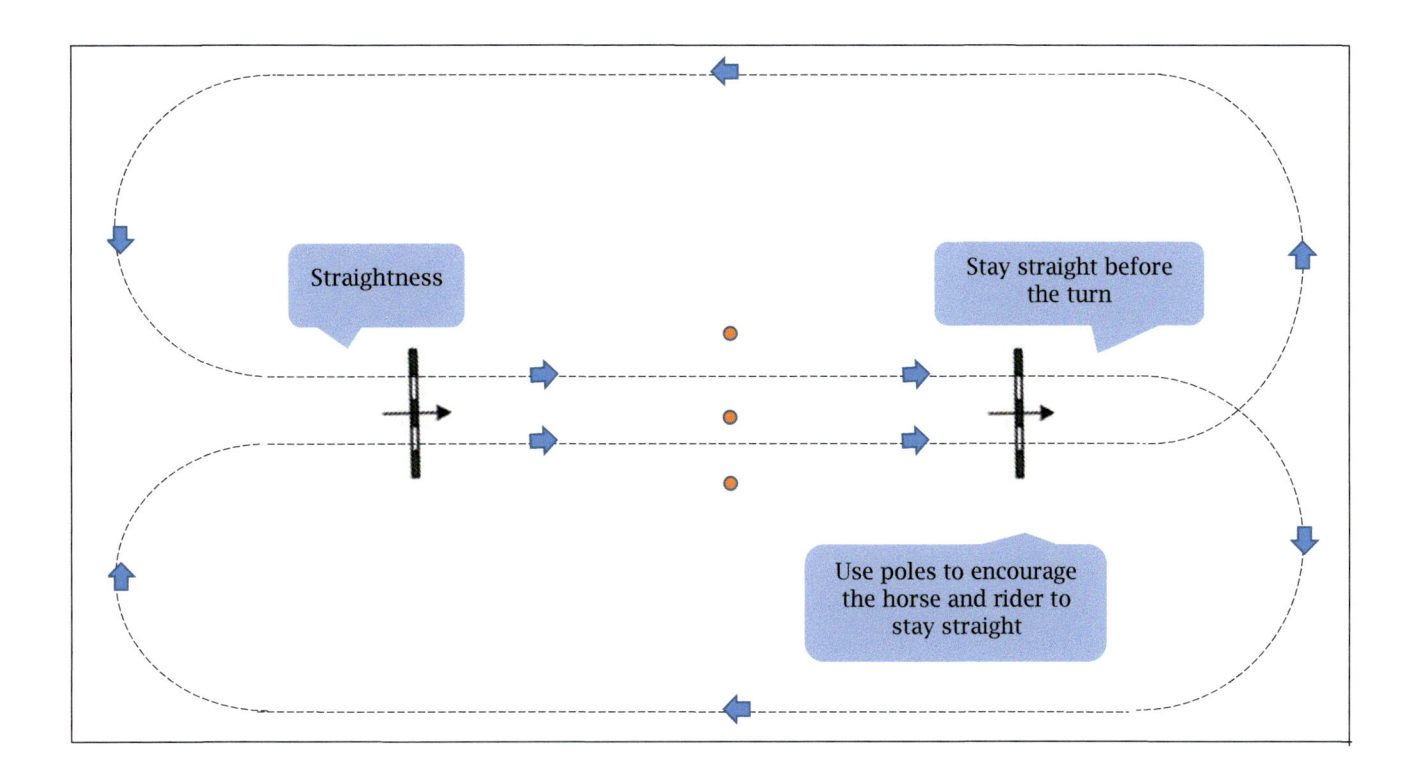

Diagram labels:
- Straightness
- Stay straight before the turn
- Use poles to encourage the horse and rider to stay straight

Place two small jumps on the centre line with three cones paced as illustrated above.

Start in canter on the left rein and turn down the centre line with the intention of approaching the left quarter of the two jumps, the cones will give you guidance. Turn right at the end of the arena and repeat, but this time plan your approach on the right quarter of both jumps and then turn left at the end of the arena.

Repeat until your turn and approach are accurate.

Aims:
- ✓ To increase rider accuracy of turns and straightness
- ✓ To improve collection and quality of canter
- ✓ To keep the rider planning ahead
- ✓ To encourage the horse to listen

Coach's tips:
- Remember to use a half-halt to balance the horse before the turns
- Be clear with your communication to the horse
- Make sure your hips and shoulders are parallel to the jump

Progression;
When you feel confident in your accuracy, remove the cones and repeat.

Exercise 25 - Riding with precision

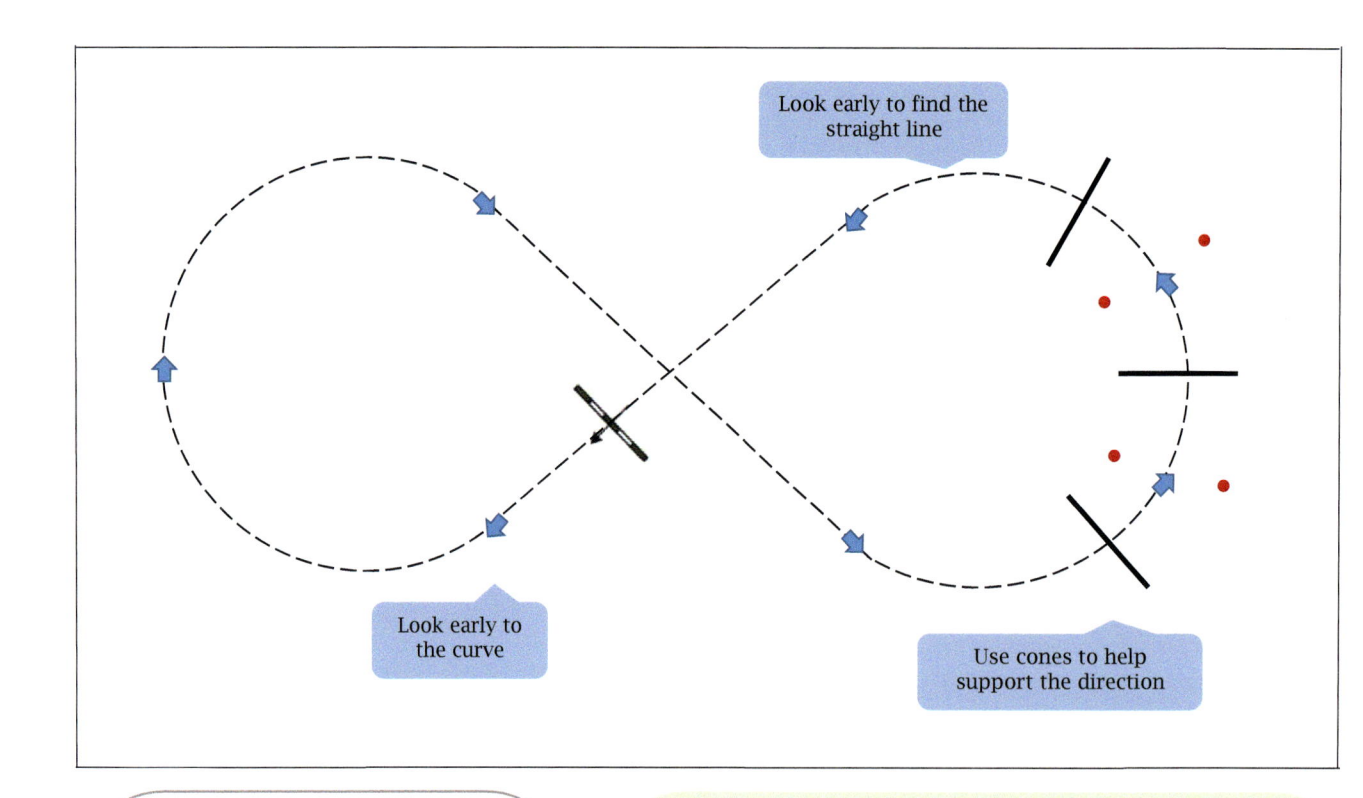

Diagram labels:
- Look early to find the straight line
- Look early to the curve
- Use cones to help support the direction

Place three poles on a curve with one canter stride between each. Then place a small jump across the diagonal.

Start in canter on the left rein over the poles, using the cones to help guide you and your horse on the curve. Then change the rein over the jump across the diagonal. Make a loop to the right, back across the diagonal before returning to the poles again.

Repeat on the opposite rein to keep your work equal.

Aims:
- ✓ To increase rider accuracy when riding a curve
- ✓ To improve collection and quality of canter
- ✓ To keep the rider planning ahead
- ✓ To encourage the horse to listen

Coach's tips:
- Keep your body balance central to the horse
- Be aware of the horse falling in or out on the curve
- Make sure your hips and shoulders are parallel to the jump

Progression:
When your curve feels accurate remove the cones to check your precision. The poles can then be changed to cavaletti stands to increase difficulty.

Exercise 25a – Riding with precision

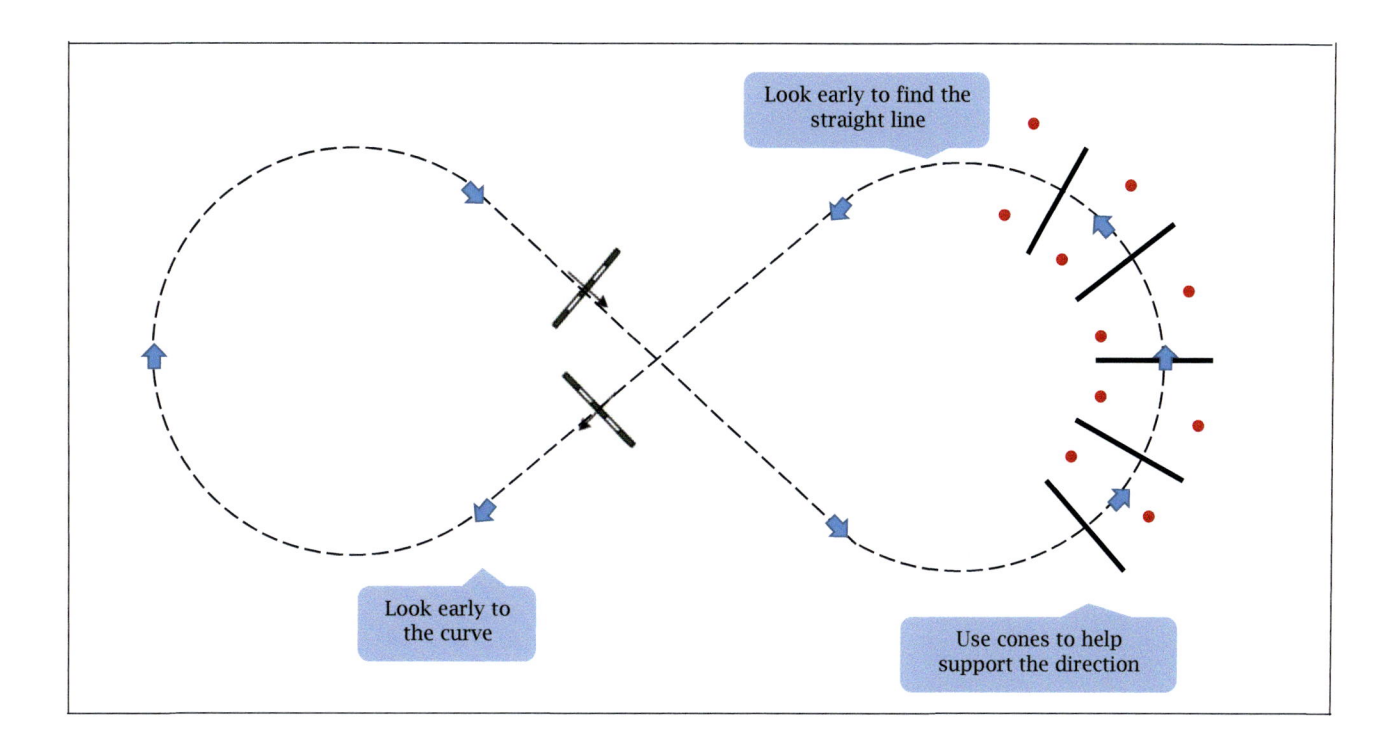

Diagram labels:
- Look early to find the straight line
- Look early to the curve
- Use cones to help support the direction

Place five canter poles on a curve, as illustrated above. Then place two small jumps across the diagonals.

Start in canter on the left rein over the canter poles, change the rein over the first jump across the diagonal.
Make a loop to the right, back across the diagonal over the second jump, before returning to the canter poles again.

Repeat on the opposite rein to keep your work equal.

Aims:
- ✓ To increase rider accuracy when riding a curve
- ✓ To improve collection and quality of canter
- ✓ To keep the rider planning ahead
- ✓ To encourage the horse to use his back and be supple

Coach's tips:
- Remember to use a half-halt to balance the horse before the turns
- Be aware of the horse falling in or out on the curve
- Use a light seat to allow the horse to use his back on the curve

Progression:
When your curve feels accurate remove the cones to check your precision. The poles can then be changed to cavaletti stands to increase difficulty.

Exercise 25b - Riding with precision

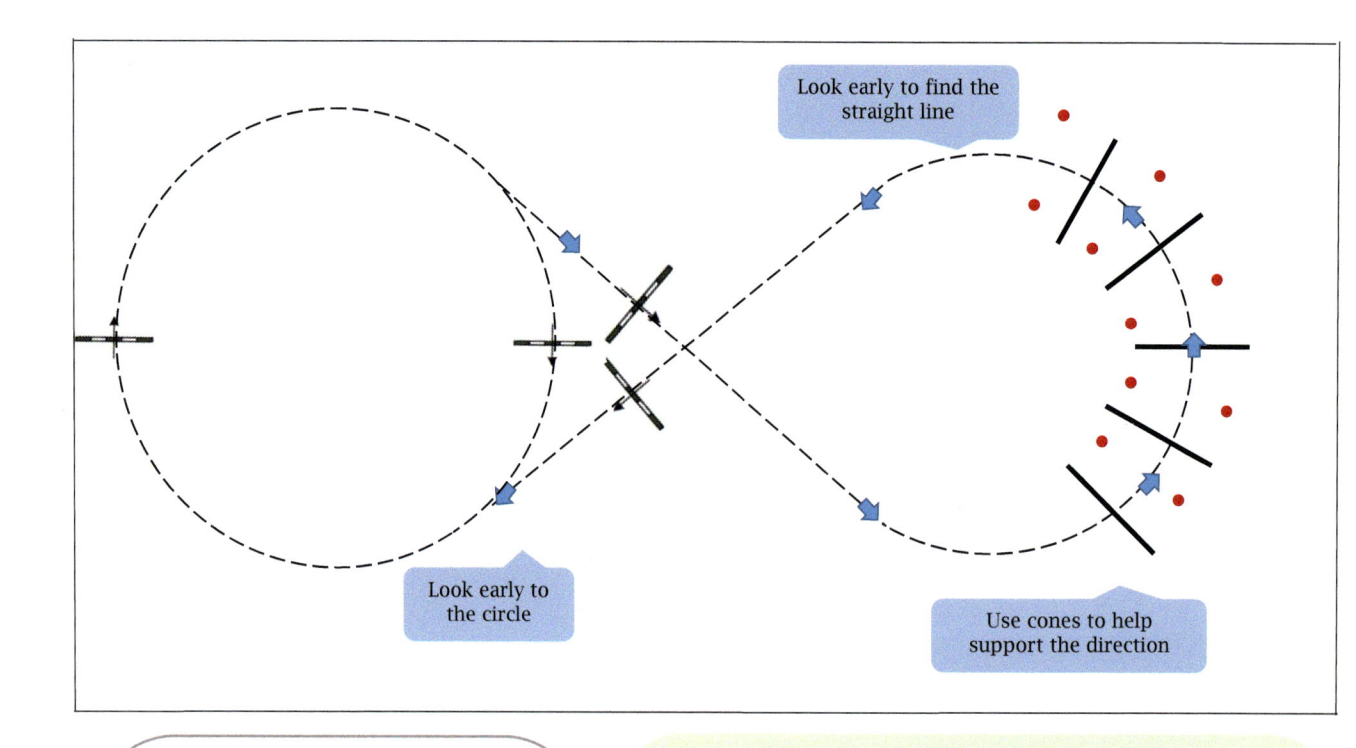

Labels in diagram:
- Look early to find the straight line
- Look early to the circle
- Use cones to help support the direction

Place five canter poles on a curve, two small jumps across the diagonals, and two further jumps on the circle, as illustrated above.

Start at canter on the left rein over the canter poles, then change the rein over the jump across the diagonal before circling right over the next two jumps. Change the rein again across the diagonal over the final jump, before returning to the canter poles again to finish.

Repeat on the opposite rein to keep your work equal.

Aims:
- To increase rider accuracy when riding curves, circles and straight lines
- To improve collection and quality of canter
- To keep the rider planning ahead
- To encourage the horse to use his back and be supple

Coach's tips:
- Keep your focus on the next movement
- Be aware of the horse falling in or out on the curve
- Don't let the exercise feel rushed, give your horse time to learn

Progression:
When your curve feels accurate remove the cones to check your precision. The poles can then be changed to cavaletti stands to increase difficulty.

I hope you have enjoyed, been motivated, and benefitted from all the exercises in this book.

Mandy Frost